The Black Archive

LOVE & MONSTERS

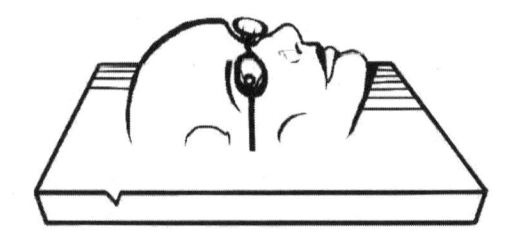

By Niki Haringsma

Published February 2019 by Obverse Books

Cover Design © Cody Schell

Text © Niki Haringsma, 2019

Range Editors: Paul Simpson, Philip Purser-Hallard

Niki Haringsma has asserted the right to be identified as the author of this Work in accordance with the Copyright, Designs and Patents Act 1988.

All rights reserved. No part of this publication may be reproduced, stored in a retrieval system, or in any form or by any means, without the prior permission in writing of the publisher, nor be otherwise circulated in any form of binding, cover or e-book other than which it is published and without a similar condition including this condition being imposed on the subsequent publisher.

For Dave

CONTENTS

Overview

Synopsis

Chapter 1: 'I Had to Invent this Rudimentary Pulley System'

Chapter 2: 'Spaceships and Lasers and Everything'

Chapter 3: 'This Isn't, You Know, My Whole Life'

Chapter 4: 'Great Big Absorbing Creature from Outer Space'

Chapter 5: 'We've Got the Place to Ourselves'

Chapter 6: 'Fetch a Spade!'

Chapter 7: 'What He Never Won't Represent'

Conclusion

Afterword

Bibliography

Acknowledgements

Biography

OVERVIEW

Serial Title: *Love & Monsters*

Writer: Russell T Davies

Director: Dan Zeff

Original UK Transmission Date: 17 June 2006

Running Time: 45m 05s

UK Viewing Figure: 6.7 million

Regular Cast: David Tennant (The Doctor), Billie Piper (Rose)

Recurring Cast: Camille Coduri (Jackie Tyler)

Guest Cast: Peter Kay (Victor Kennedy / The Abzorbaloff), Marc Warren (Elton Pope), Shirley Henderson (Ursula Blake), Simon Greenall (Mr Skinner), Moya Brady (Bridget), Kathryn Drysdale (Bliss), Paul Kasey (The Hoix), Bella Emberg (Mrs Croot)

Antagonist: The Abzorbaloff

Responses:

'[A]n episode even less coherent and even more given to whiplash-inducing tonal shifts than *Boom Town*, which was never a story noted for its narrative consistency.'

[Alasdair Wilkins, *AV Club*]

'Those that can look past the absurdity and embrace the fantastic dialogue will thoroughly enjoy this episode from start to finish.'

[Ahsan Haque, *IGN*]

SYNOPSIS

A young man, **Elton Pope**, seems to recognise the TARDIS when he sees it outside a warehouse, but when he meets **the Doctor** and **Rose** as they tackle a Hoix, he runs away in panic. Later, he relates his story to a video camera.

As a young child, he found the Doctor in his house, and later he was caught up in the chaos caused by the Auton, Slitheen and Sycorax invasions. When he started to investigate them, he discovered the Doctor was involved and met a group of others (**Ursula Blake**, **Bliss**, **Bridget Sinclair** and **Colin Skinner**) also seeking the Time Lord. Elton dubs them LINDA – the London Investigation 'N' Detective Agency. The members of LINDA are as happy socialising as searching for the Doctor, until the arrival of **Victor Kennedy**, a wealthy Northern gentleman who claims he suffers from 'exeema' and cannot be touched. He pushes them to find the Doctor – leading to Elton's encounter at the warehouse.

After Elton's perceived cowardice, Kennedy decides to find the Doctor by targeting Rose, sending Elton to get information from her mother, **Jackie**. Elton and Jackie get on well, but after hearing Jackie talking to Rose on the phone, Elton is ashamed of trying to use her, and realises he loves Ursula. When Jackie finds a photo of Rose in Elton's jacket, she tells him to leave her alone since it's clear his only interest in her was to get to Rose.

Elton tells Kennedy that he's ruined LINDA – those that are left, anyway: both Bridget and Bliss have recently mysteriously disappeared. Kennedy offers to help Mr Skinner find Bridget, but when Ursula and Elton return to collect Ursula's phone, they discover that Kennedy is in fact a huge green alien who has just absorbed Mr

Skinner, having previously absorbed the two women. **The Abzorbaloff**, as Elton nicknames him, is after the Doctor.

As Ursula threatens to beat the Abzorbaloff with his own cane, the creature manages to absorb her, and her face ends up on its chest (the other two victims are elsewhere on its body). She tells Elton to run to avoid a similar fate, and the Abzorbaloff chases after him. The TARDIS materialises, with Rose furious at Elton over the way he treated her mother. The Doctor interrogates the Abzorbaloff, who is a native of Clom, the twin planet of Raxacoricofallapatorius. At Ursula's urging, now she can read the alien's mind, Elton snaps the cane and the Abzorbaloff dissolves into a liquid goo – along with all those inside it.

The Doctor explains to Elton that when they first met, he was hunting a living shadow that killed Elton's mother. He saves Elton again by partially restoring Ursula; however, she will forever be a face in a paving stone (although they can have a bit of a love life). Later, Elton reflects on his meetings with the Doctor; he brings death and destruction to those he comes in contact with – how long will it be before Rose and Jackie are affected?

CHAPTER 1: 'I HAD TO INVENT THIS RUDIMENTARY PULLEY SYSTEM'
The Art of Double-Banking

In June 2006, *Love & Monsters* was broadcast for the first time. It was a bold experiment: an adventure just barely starring the Doctor and Rose, designed to be recorded at the same time as the two-part story preceding it.

The recording schedule for the previous season had been so strict that filming of *The Long Game* and *The Empty Child / The Doctor Dances* (all 2005) had overlapped. The amount of stress that this put on the production team was something neither Executive Producer Russell T Davies nor the BBC wanted to repeat. But the last-minute addition of a Christmas special to the 2006 recording schedule meant that 14 episodes needed to be filmed in the period reserved for 13 – giving the team even less time than in the previous year to produce each story. To work around this problem, Davies decided that for episode 2.10, he would minimise the appearances of the Doctor and Rose. This allowed David Tennant and Billie Piper to record their *Love & Monsters* scenes in the middle of filming *The Impossible Planet / The Satan Pit* (2006)[1].

Davies was directly inspired by the episode *The Zeppo* (1999) of Joss Whedon's TV series **Buffy the Vampire Slayer** (1997-2003), in which the regular cast's adventures were viewed from the sidelines. He decided to focus on everyday events while the expected sci-fi

---

[1] ***Doctor Who**: The Complete History Volume 53*, p50.

adventures took a backseat[2]. It was a format never before used in **Doctor Who**. Davies liked the results, and the 'Doctor-lite' and 'companion-lite' episodes would become a continuing feature of the show during his tenure. *Love & Monsters* was a testing ground for this technique, figuring out the balance between story elements that could keep **Doctor Who** engaging even without its hero there.

The episode brought in a new batch of characters to replace the leads: the geeky everyman Elton Pope, the determined Ursula, the free-spirited Bliss, the calm Mr Skinner and the melancholy Bridget. They were for the most part one-note characters, stock figures with scraps of personality stapled to their frames. But together, they formed a group that became more than the sum of its parts – LINDA, the London Investigation 'N' Detective Agency. This gang ended up a lot like our own fandom in their efforts to experience the Doctor's world.

Most of the episode was shot on location so that a second unit could simultaneously film the final scenes of *The Impossible Planet / The Satan Pit*. Marc Warren recorded his adventures as Elton while Tennant and Piper were off facing Ood. The brief encounters between their two worlds, which bookend the story, were shot with Tennant and Piper being shipped back and forth between sets in a hurry[3].

The episode's squeeze extended beyond its filming schedule – it was also given an unusually tight budget. A handful of location sets were combined with sparse CGI frames and music which recalled cues

---

[2] *Love & Monsters* DVD commentary.
[3] *The Complete History* #53, p58.

from the 2005 series. This left enough money for other, less Earth-bound episodes in the season to go all out with special effects and extravagant scenery[4].

The episode's writing and directing drew on the atmosphere of Red Production Company shows like **Clocking Off** (2000-03), **Bob & Rose** (2001) and **Linda Green** (2001-02). These series had involved several of the people who would go on to create *Love & Monsters* (e.g. Davies, actor Marc Warren, producer Phil Collinson, composer Murray Gold and director Dan Zeff) and showcased the lives of ordinary working-class people against recognisable backdrops. The quirky style of Davies' work with Red Production Company, which could flip from cartoonish comedy to serious human drama at a moment's notice, became the template for LINDA's story.

And so, Elton's world wasn't one of outer space adventures or breath-taking futures, but instead took us to basements, launderettes and slightly dirty alleyways. A monster thrown into the opening scene was cobbled together from leftover prosthetics and given the name 'Hoix' only as a credits sequence afterthought[5]. The episode's overall look was shabby – in part due to time and budget constraints, and in part because the production decided to embrace the cheap aesthetic and to emphasise a dingy, everyday atmosphere. For these 45 minutes, viewers were shut out of the show's space-exploring premise and instead got served a bunch of nerds sitting on old chairs and shaking tambourines.

Love & Monsters ended up with a reputation of being marmite –

---

[4] *The Complete History* #53, p60.
[5] *Love & Monsters* DVD commentary.

either you love it or you hate it. But where some other episodes had become bywords for dull, cheaply-produced or badly-acted **Doctor Who**, *Love & Monsters* wasn't so easily defined. It was Doctor-lite, but never dull. Its production was cheap, but there were no bad CSO shots or wobbly walls to mock. And its acting was at times broad, but nowhere near the hammy glory of decades past. The story's infamy was instead sparked by the way it treated **Doctor Who**'s own fandom – and by its irreverent, gaudy, and at times absolutely disgusting imagery.

The episode was something entirely new for **Who**. It treated the Doctor as a stranger, it broke the show's format, and it took the fans on a trip they never bargained for. And in everything that made it so unique, it invited a closer look at its inner workings. So let's dive in…

CHAPTER 2: 'SPACESHIPS AND LASERS AND EVERYTHING'

Intertextuality and Narrative Technique

In most televised episodes, the Doctor and the companions serve as our viewpoint characters. We experience the story by their side. A double-banked episode needs a replacement of these elements, so Elton Pope fills that gap, guiding us through a single story before leaving the series again by the episode's end. Due to Elton's limited knowledge, we end up excluded from the action that would usually make up a **Doctor Who** episode.

This fresh view on the show causes a double shift in perspective. On the one hand, the audience is used to the viewpoints of the Doctor and the companions; suddenly, we're invited to see their adventures through the eyes of an outsider. On the other hand, we view Elton's adventures through our knowledge of the Doctor's world. Because of this, we see the Doctor through Elton just as we see Elton through our expectations of **Doctor Who**. The result is an interplay between perspectives which puts the viewer on both sides of the narrative at once.

In his writing on narratives, literary scholar Jörg Helbig discusses how a story can place a protagonist outside of the usual context, which can shift them away from the expected dynamic between authors, characters and audiences. This way of storytelling, Helbig explains, allows for a change in power: a dominant hero can become a side character, and a minor element can influence the viewer in ways usually reserved for the protagonist[6]. The author playfully invites the audience to experience familiar things in a new light. This effect is even stronger when the fictional nature of the story is (implicitly or explicitly) pointed out. Helbig calls this method an intertextual 'game'[7]: an appropriate way to describe the silly tone of *Love & Monsters*.

We enter the episode's plot at a breakneck pace together with Elton. As he runs into the world of **Doctor Who**, we hear the voices of Rose and the Doctor, already up to their necks in an adventure. It's telling that their voices, not their faces, announce their presence: this allows the camera to stay on Elton, establishing him as our focus.

It takes him just over a minute to become immersed in recognisable bits of the Doctor's adventures, facing a classic corridor and hearing a monster in its hiding place. And just as quickly, without the scene even showing us the Doctor, Elton is cast out of the world of **Doctor Who** again as we cut to him sitting at home, telling an audience about what he saw.

This setup in which Elton tries (and miserably fails) to become part of the Doctor's life is continued once the flashback resumes, when we see the Doctor physically shutting the door on him. We get a brief moment of the Doctor stopping in his tracks to talk to Elton before our new narrator runs off, taking us along with him, away from the adventure and back into everyday life. The game aspect described by Helbig is in full force here: the dynamic between Elton and the world

---

[6] Helbig, Jörg, *Intertextualität und Markierung* ['Intertextuality and Marking'], p113. Unless otherwise noted, all translations of German media are my own.
[7] Helbig, *Intertextualität und Markierung*, p93.

of **Doctor Who** is a cat-and-mouse game, and Davies takes the viewer along for the ride in a gleefully playful way.

The recording symbols on the screen, the slightly warped edges of the video image and the explicit reference to the camera make it clear that Elton's addressing an in-universe audience. But since this fictional audience stays unseen, it's left to us — the viewers — to embody them. 'Don't worry,' Elton reassures his in-story audience, "cause it's not just me sitting here talking.' Although Elton stays unaware of any audience outside of the fourth wall, these words also invite **Doctor Who**'s viewers to consider themselves addressed by him. Again, we're presented with the two different viewpoints at once. As Elton's in-universe audience, we become familiar with the Doctor's world through his narration; while as ourselves, we see Elton's life through our knowledge of the show.

This creates a much more metafictional style of storytelling than in other TV episodes of the Davies era[8]. Even when the Doctor talks to an in-universe camera in *Blink* (2007), the presence of temporary main character Sally Sparrow enforces the idea that it's her, not us, being addressed. Only when the 12th Doctor developed a habit of talking to the camera directly, with no one that he could be addressing in-universe, did our presence as viewers become even more tangible[9].

---

[8] Only surpassed by the red button TV minisode game 'Attack of the Graske' (2005), in which the viewer becomes the Doctor's companion in first-person perspective.

[9] Seen for example in *Listen* (2014), *Before The Flood* (2015) and *Heaven Sent* (2015) plus countless silent glances at the camera throughout his seasons. While the fourth wall has been poked at or

The next glimpse of the Doctor is seen in another flashback: a distorted memory from Elton's childhood[10]. This one's also cut short, another indication that *Love & Monsters* is about Elton's experiences instead of focusing on the Doctor and Rose. As if to cement this, the same visual is repeated twice more in ever-shorter form. From this point on until the story's final minutes, any image we see of the Doctor or Rose is shown either as a repetition of previous scenes or as media that the characters share with each other.

Elton proceeds to tell his audience that he was present for the events of *Rose, Aliens of London* and *The Christmas Invasion* (all 2005), with new footage emphasising his role as someone who shows us the perspective of the sidelines. We're told that he has been peripheral to the plot, as an unseen pair of eyes, from the day the Doctor was first re-introduced to 2005's viewer base.

Estrangement as a Storytelling Device

This kind of estrangement can make an audience look at stories in whole new ways. The Russian literary scholar Viktor Shklovsky explored this exact estrangement (as the neologism 'ostrannenye'[11])

---

broken on other occasions in **Doctor Who**, the 12th Doctor made this into a continuous character trait.

[10] This nested structure of Elton reflecting on past events is most succinctly summarised by Andrew Pixley: 'There were then 33 flashbacks.' *The Complete History* #53, p55.

[11] Spelled at first by Shklovsky as остранение and subsequently as остраннение, a new word constructed from roots which can mean 'strange' and 'to the side'; also Romanised as ostraniene, ostranenye, ostrannenie and so on; variously translated as defamiliarisation, alienation and **en**strangement as well.

from 1913 onwards in his narrative theories.

'By "estranging" objects and complicating form,' Shklovsky stated, 'the device of art makes perception long and "laborious". The perceptual process in art has a purpose all its own and ought to be extended to the fullest.' This means that familiar things can be described as if they're new and unfamiliar, to uncover aspects which are often overlooked. Through an unexpected viewpoint character, a writer can de-automate the audience's perceptions. According to Shklovsky, this works especially well for 'eternal' stories such as fables (or, say, long-running franchises) which become so recognisable over time that the audience slips into an uncritical, automised way of looking at them[12].

Shklovsky's contemporary, the German playwright Bertolt Brecht, explored this same idea with his own theory of the estrangement effect ('Verfremdungseffekt', also translated as alienation effect or defamiliarisation effect). Brecht deliberately alienated audiences from familiar things. His plays were populated largely by allegorical stock figures, instead of by characters with intricate thoughts or backgrounds. What he called dialectical theatre ('dialectical' as in societal dialogue) presented a change from the dramatic theatre forms that were common at the time.

Brecht summarised these changes as follows[13]:

---

[12] Shklovsky, Viktor, *Theory of Prose*, p6.
[13] Paraphrased by me from Brecht, Bertolt and Peter Suhrkamp, 'Anmerkungen zur Oper *Aufstieg und Fall der Stadt Mahagonny*' ['Notes on the opera "Rise and Fall of the City of Mahagonny"'] in Kraft, Peter et al, eds, *Bertolt Brecht: Schriften 4* ['Writings 4'], p74ff; Brecht, Bertolt, 'Kleines Organon für das Theater' ['Short Organum

Dramatic narratives	Dialectical narratives
The focus lies on actions.	The focus lies on the way a story is told.
The viewer is immersed in the story.	The viewer is made into an observer and confronted with subjective, unreliable interpretations of the story.
The audience is ignored by the storytelling.	The audience is involved in the storytelling.
Human nature is treated as a given.	Human nature is investigated from a new perspective.
The focus lies on people as they are.	The focus lies on people's social roles being transformed, and on the ways in which they themselves can transform others.

for the Theatre'] in Wallburg, Barbara et al, *Bertolt Brecht: Schriften 3* ['Writings 3'], p65-97; Brecht, Bertolt, 'Nachträge zum "Kleinen Organon"' ['Addenda to the "Short Organum"'] in *Schriften 3*, p289-295; and Barnett, David, *Brecht in Practice: Theatre, Theory and Performance*. Brecht originally termed this type of theatre 'epic' (as in narrated journey) and switched to 'dialectical' later in his life.

Dramatic narratives	Dialectical narratives
The characters' consistent emotions make them into realistic persons.	The figures are realistic not because of emotional consistency, but because they respond unexpectedly to different circumstances.
The characters are defined by their backstories and personalities.	The figures are defined by their choices within the story.
The story's dialogue is presented as-is.	Ironic, unreliable narration or other multimedial elements contradict the story's dialogue.
The events are shown as they happen.	The events are shown from the perspective of someone telling the story to someone else.
Audiences are invited to directly empathise with the characters' actions, which are presented as logical parts of the plot.	Audiences are invited to treat the figures' actions as unnecessary choices (influenced by society's contradictory demands), and to come up with alternative solutions (involving social change).

Dramatic narratives	Dialectical narratives
The characters resist their circumstances and strive to overcome them.	The figures accept their circumstances to an uncomfortable degree, which invites spectators to think about how they themselves would respond differently.
All of the elements are in line: e.g. a scary scene has scary music, scary lights and scary dialogue.	All of the elements can contradict each other: e.g. a scary scene can have exciting music, bright lights and silly dialogue.
Scenes are presented as an organic continuum: each part leads into the next.	Each scene is a standalone piece, and the story jumps between these disjointed and contradictory parts, which together form a montage.
Audiences can follow the story by just watching.	Audiences must piece together the story and the figures' motivations by watching critically.

Dramatic narratives	Dialectical narratives
The ending is the most important narrative segment.	The journey towards the ending is more important than the resolution.
The ending resolves the story.	The ending leaves key questions unresolved, inviting the viewer to think about what could happen next.

Brecht emphasised that this change from dramatic to dialectical theatre wasn't a strict contrast, but that the two forms could instead mark different sides of a spectrum. His goal in writing dialectical stories was to make audiences look critically at the world around them and at their own role as receptive viewers. By making his audiences into observers, and his characters into figures who were constantly transformed by their positions in society, he wanted to convey that real-life society could be transformed as well – and that keen viewers could be the ones to make this change happen.

These differences between dramatic and dialectical theatre map quite well onto the shift from common-or-garden-variety **Doctor Who** to *Love & Monsters*. Of course, as a whole, the series covers all points on this spectrum, and shifts between styles at a moment's notice. *The Impossible Planet / The Satan Pit* and *Fear Her*, which surround *Love & Monsters* in the 2006 series, are all told in chronological order and stay close to the conventions of drama which *Love & Monsters* chooses to subvert instead.

While Elton narrates for us, his observing audience, we keep jumping between disjointed chunks of plot. This prevents the level of immersion that we're used to. And the idea of characters as transformative and transformed becomes literal as the Abzorbaloff and LINDA – particularly Ursula – invite critical questions about humanity, identity and agency.

Brecht, like Shklovsky, strongly valued stories in which familiar things are looked at through a new pair of eyes. When he and his partner Elisabeth Hauptmann first presented their famous stage play *The Threepenny Opera* (1928), its disjointed format estranged audiences who were used to straightforward theatre. The dialectical format gave their fans a fresh perspective, and presented a story in which disenfranchised people addressed how they viewed the unjust world around them.

There are interesting parallels between the *Threepenny* mythos and *Love & Monsters*. The plot of *The Threepenny Opera* was sparse and stripped bare of any pomp or glamour. The sardonic writing revolved around needy and love-struck people trying to get by in a harsh world that didn't want them. They did so while being swindled by a fascist gangster boss figure, Macheath, nicknamed Mack the Knife. All of the elements on stage were designed to be confrontational and uncomfortable, as reflections of what was wrong in the world outside the play.

To this end, the songs in *The Threepenny Opera* were dissonant, the sets looked cheap, the flimsy figures made bad mistakes, and the happy ending was deliberately implausible and jarring. But Brecht ended up dissatisfied with the play's reception: although all the main figures were meant as morally questionable in the face of Germany's rising fascism, and as examples of how **not** to act, audiences just saw them as fun and entertaining[14].

In response, Brecht rewrote the play into *Threepenny Novel* (1934) to present an alternative take on the story. The book version added a new viewpoint figure, an ordinary man called Fewkoombey, on the existing narrative's sidelines. This enabled yet another level of estrangement and showed how the actions of *The Threepenny Opera*'s familiar figures negatively affected the lives of Fewkoombey and other regular people.

The Threepenny Novel's re-telling of the play asks the readers to question the knowledge they already have, by providing new information about the existing story. Much of this is presented using in-universe media such as books, newspapers and camera recordings; **seemingly** neutral devices which, like the figures' actions, audiences are also invited to question. Readers enter and leave the new narrative structure together with Fewkoombey, who barely interacts with the familiar main figures but whose life ends up ruined by their actions. As the readers are cast out from the plot again by the end, they're asked to be critical of everything and to draw their own conclusions.

Brecht's goal was to make readers shake off automatic reception by confronting them with these alienating new elements. Everything in

---

[14] Schutte, Jürgen, *Einführung in die Literaturinterpretation*, p157. In the interest of historical accuracy: the *Threepenny* mythos has a more complicated background than these two stories alone, having been adapted by Hauptmann from John Gay's play *The Beggar's Opera* and subsequently expanded on by Brecht.

the book was presented as unreliable. He meant for his readers to actively engage with the storytelling and to relate Fewkoombey's perspective to real-life society, transforming the negative experiences and actions of the characters into positive sociopolitical actions in their own everyday lives[15].

Love & Monsters similarly makes us see the Doctor's familiar world from the viewpoint of – as the shooting script calls Elton – 'a nice, ordinary bloke – not a twat'[16]. Elton's role is like Fewkoombey's: a new guy jarringly finding his footing in an existing framework.

There are other interesting parallels between *Love & Monsters* and Brecht:

- *Love & Monsters* shows us **Doctor Who** through Elton's eyes and camera, and nudges us toward adopting an in-universe identity. The narration of *The Threepenny Novel* similarly places readers close to Fewkoombey by describing him with words like 'here' and 'us'[17].
- Elton's viewpoint states that the Hoix chase looks cartoonish, a clue that his story may be embellished. Brecht emphasised the fictionality of his scenes with stylised physical exaggerations, to keep the audience

---

[15] Brecht, Bertolt, '[Aufgeben der Einfühlung]' ['[Letting Go of Immersion]'] in Gellert, Inge et al, eds, *Bertolt Brecht: Schriften 2* ['Writings 2'], p174ff.
[16] *The Complete History* #53, p54.
[17] Schutte, *Einführung in die Literaturinterpretation*, p157.

critical and to prevent unquestioning immersion[18].

- LINDA view the Doctor through seemingly neutral media such as camera recordings. These technologies are unreliable due to the Bad Wolf 'virus', which has corrupted data about Rose throughout history[19]. (The 2005 episode *Bad Wolf* itself is, fittingly, partly about untrustworthy media.) Recording technology is presented as unreliable in Brecht's stories as well, as something to question precisely because of its reputation of neutrality.
- Elton addresses us across the divide between fiction and reality (albeit unknowingly). Brecht's characters are happy to break the fourth wall and talk to the audience directly.
- We stay to hear Elton's thoughts until the credits roll, rather than going back to the TARDIS with the Doctor and Rose. The *Threepenny Novel*'s final chapter centres on Fewkoombey's philosophical musings, though the plot is long since over with.
- LINDA show the lives of regular humans, far away from the pomp and glamour of space travel. Brecht wrote about the outcasts, the unlucky, banding together to

---

[18] Brecht, Bertolt, 'Zu *Die Mutter*' ['On *The Mother*'] in *Schriften 4*, p155. Also examined in Schutte, *Einführung in die Literaturinterpretation*, p62. For more on the reliability of Elton's narrative, see Chapter 3.

[19] A more practical reason for the corrupted media files was Davies needing to explain why Torchwood mistook Jackie for Rose in *Army Of Ghosts* (2006). *The Complete History* #53, p54.

- forge their own happiness.
- In the guise of Victor Kennedy, the Abzorbaloff mirrors the wealthy capitalist villain stereotype of Brechtian writing embodied by Mack the Knife, becoming every bit the ruthless, gluttonous 'robber baron' of anti-capitalist discourse that the little people in Brecht's worlds are encouraged to stand up against. As Brecht, a rather dedicated Marxist, put it: '[...] fascism can only be battled as capitalism, as the most naked, most shameless, most oppressive and most treacherous capitalism.'[20]

In *Love & Monsters*, to quote critic Jon Arnold, 'we see not only the visible consequences of the Doctor's adventures but the invisible ones too'. These are the emotional scars, 'the weight those left behind have to carry'[21]: the impact on all the Fewkoombeys on the sidelines of the show.

Aside from parallels with Brecht, a comparison to Tom Stoppard's *Rosencrantz And Guildenstern are Dead* also comes to mind. Davies mentions this absurdist 1966 play in his wide-ranging interview with Toby Hadoke as a direct influence on *Love & Monsters*[22].

Stoppard's play shows Shakespeare's *Hamlet* entirely from the perspective of the two titular men. Their status as minor characters in the original story is dissected as they stumble clumsily through

---

[20] Brecht, Bertolt, 'Fünf Schwierigkeiten beim Schreiben der Wahrheit' ['Five Difficulties in Writing the Truth'] in *Schriften 2*, p78.
[21] Arnold, Jon, 'Love & Monsters', in Southall, JR, ed, *Hating to Love: Re-Evaluating the 52 Worst **Doctor Who** Stories of All Time*, p103.
[22] **Toby Hadoke's Who's Round** #99, 'Russell T Davies: Part 4'.

their plot. Having been granted just enough identity by Stoppard to feed the actual main characters the right lines, they know almost nothing about their own world. They only catch the occasional glimpse of *Hamlet*'s narrative framework, which the audience freely has access to.

Like Brecht's Fewkoombey and like the LINDA gang, these unexpected viewpoint characters try – and fail – to make sense of the larger story that they find themselves inserted into. Rosencrantz and Guildenstern tolerate their eventual doom, because it's decided outside of their hands by the true protagonists and by the larger story surrounding them, similarly to how Elton and Ursula accept their own ending with resignation.

On another narrative level, we could also see ourselves as being similar to Rosencrantz and Guildenstern while we're Elton's camcorder audience. Much like the two hapless men, we have no idea who we're meant to be within the fiction, what we're named, where we came from, how we got there, or what we're supposed to do. The plot as narrated by Elton appears fragmented, providing only those segments which are deemed relevant to us.

In discussing *Love & Monsters*, Davies states that he was also inspired by the **Star Trek: The Next Generation** (1987-94) episode *Lower Decks* (1994), which follows the same structure as Stoppard's play and was instrumental in spreading this trope to science fiction[23]. *Lower Decks* showed **The Next Generation's** setting and plot from the perspectives of minor crew members, who stayed unaware of

---

[23] *Love & Monsters* DVD commentary. The episode's influence includes becoming the trope namer on TV Tropes, where this narrative style is referred to as a 'Lower-Deck Episode'.

the series' larger narrative even as they continued to be affected by it.

Davies talks about his love for these 'little people' who show up for just one story, and of his delight as a child when Target novelisations of **Doctor Who** episodes would spotlight these figures[24]. This focus on intimate, very human events plus the excision of common storytelling aspects is a technique Davies uses often. He adores stories in which major narrative elements are skipped over, much like the way Rosencrantz and Guildenstern experience their plot, to focus on everyday character moments instead:

> 'If you take out the drama, then what's left becomes very, very dramatic. [...] Let's avoid the problem, let's avoid the confrontation, let's just keep going with Elton. Keep him bumbling along, 'cause it's more interesting to keep him in his bedroom. He hasn't inherited a castle in the end, he doesn't travel in time and space with the Doctor in the end. He's just sitting there with his paving stone. And yes, his life is a thousand times more dramatic than if he was Prince of Mars.'[25]

LINDA, Fewkoombey, Rosencrantz and Guildenstern and **The Next Generation**'s lower deck crew are all part of this same storytelling tradition: their tales invite us to come sit for a while with all the people who usually end up ignored.

---

[24] **Toby Hadoke's Who's Round** #54, 'Russell T Davies: Part 2'.
[25] **Toby Hadoke's Who's Round** #124, 'Russell T Davies: Part 5'.

The One-Off Narrator

When a new audience surrogate is introduced, their perspective forges a bond between them, the Doctor, and the audience. The character's experiences bridge the gap between our own lives and the near-limitless universe that the Doctor travels. This puts the Doctor's journeys into a framework we can easily understand. The classic example, of schoolteachers Ian and Barbara meeting the Doctor in *An Unearthly Child* (1963), takes the audience from their everyday lives into the world of the series. As they move from a familiar school setting into IM Foreman's junkyard and through the TARDIS doors, we walk alongside them into the fantastical.

The same technique was later successfully repeated by Davies in *Rose* and by Executive Producers Steven Moffat and Chris Chibnall in *The Pilot* (2017) and *The Woman Who Fell to Earth* (2018). These episodes were designed to establish the Doctor for a modern audience through the eyes of relatable, everyday companions. *The Woman Who Fell to Earth* even gave us another Elton-ish vlog format in Ryan's narration, albeit briefly.

Narratives like these focus on creating connections between all the elements that are present: the Doctor, the companion(s), the audience, the everyday, the strange, and the adventure itself. We're invited to experience the story alongside the new traveller(s), and to consider the Doctor through the lens of their personal values. These stories can be told without showing the Doctor's perspective, sometimes deliberately not giving us a moment alone with our hero. The technique provides a sense of alienation and mystery.

The audience surrogate characters typically become companions to the Doctor after the story's end – transplanting the newly forged links between all these elements into the series proper. *Love & Monsters* subverts this. The sympathetic link that exists between the viewpoint character and the audience is set up, anchored and severed in the space of one single broadcast[26]. Various stories outside of the TV episodes also use this model to great effect, but at the time of this writing, the only other **Doctor Who** TV example is found in *Blink*.

More common are stories told from the viewpoint of previously established characters. In the tie-in media such stories are, for example, found in Big Finish Productions' **Companion Chronicles** and **Short Trips** audio ranges. In addition to third-person prose, these ranges sometimes include first-person narratives told to an in-universe audience (much like Elton's) by the Doctor's friends. The Doctor's thoughts and actions in this format are only shown as interpreted by established companions.

As Shklovsky once described, it's a technique that very effectively imposes alienation from the main character on 'us, who are separated from him by the narrator'[27]. The audience of such a **Doctor Who** story is expected to be familiar with said narrators and to have formed an emotional attachment to them in advance of hearing each story (or at the very least, to have the chance to become familiar with them in other adventures). Because of this, even though the Doctor is one step removed from the listener, there's still an existing sympathetic link between the narrator and the audience, as well as

---

[26] Considering the fannish nature of LINDA, it's interesting to note that another space in which original viewpoint characters really thrive is fanfiction – see also Chapter 4.
[27] Shklovsky, *Theory of Prose*, p112.

a sense of familiarity. This contrasts with narratives like *Love & Monsters* and *Blink*, in which the connection between the audience and the viewpoint character is limited to one adventure.

Stories with unusual points of view are understood against the background of the usual structure. Each of these adventures provides a perspective on the Doctor's world that could not have been achieved through the eyes of the Doctor or the regular companions. When the new viewpoint is a one-off, we – just as we do with Brecht's Fewkoombey – enter **and** leave the story's world by their side, never quite able to walk the paths of TARDIS life.

Which begs the question: what idea does *Love & Monsters* explore that could not have been introduced from other perspectives?

Romancing the Slab

One answer is given by Davies in his **Who's Round** interview. He states that Elton symbolises alienation – specifically, the forced alienation of being gay in a heteronormative world.

What Davies calls the 'gay metaphor' relationship between Elton and Ursula alludes to the way queer relationships are sadly often judged by society as monstrous[28]. Ursula's transformation (slyly foreshadowed by ELO's song 'Turn to Stone' heard when Elton is working in Jackie's house) serves to code their relationship as queer regardless of their actual orientations. But 'I don't care what anyone thinks,' Elton tells us defiantly. 'I love her.'

This adds a tremendously interesting vibe to the story. Elton is positioned as the quintessential outsider. He's excluded from the

---

[28] **Toby Hadoke's Who's Round** #99.

show's narrative despite being its literal narrator for a while, and excluded from the Doctor's life despite the Doctor being a core part of his own. Since Elton serves as the audience's viewpoint for these 45 minutes, this in turn excludes the audience from the Doctor's life for the majority of the episode. In placing us by Elton's side, making us experience **Doctor Who** through his eyes, Davies symbolically gives us a taste of his own experiences as a gay man being excluded by a straight world. And in doing so, he asks his viewers to relate to this struggle.

Critic Elizabeth Sandifer poses that Elton is intentionally unsatisfying to watch, which slots neatly into this idea. She writes: 'Recognizing that the absence of the Doctor is going to create a tangible lack within the story, Davies picks a main character who will feed into that lack, making us want the Doctor.'[29]

The **Buffy** episode *The Zeppo*, which inspired *Love & Monsters*, attracted similar analyses: for example, Noel Murray of The A.V. Club praised how *The Zeppo*'s 'feelings of abandonment pervade the structure of the episode, which is filled with moments that are (intentionally) dramatically unsatisfying'[30].

Love & Monsters never explicitly tells us its reasons for leaving us unsatisfied, but that may actually be a strength – it invites us to fill in the blanks for ourselves. Even those viewers who feel abandoned and unsatisfied by the episode can still recognise those experiences **within** the episode's characters as well. This structure can make viewers reflect on their feelings and, maybe, relate to outsiders

---

[29] Sandifer, Elizabeth: 'Their Little Groups (*Love & Monsters*)'.
[30] Murray, Noel: 'Buffy The Vampire Slayer: *The Zeppo / Bad Girls / Consequences*'.

abandoned in real-life society a little more strongly as a result.

It's not easy to recognise the queerness in the *Love & Monsters*, though. Since romantic affection was already shown regardless of gender in this era of **Doctor Who**, there was no reason for viewers to look out for vague hints and allusions. It's true that in 2006's political UK landscape, mainstream TV stories still had to be somewhat under the radar with queer content. But **Who** fans weren't primed to expect queer issues being sneakily embodied by a male-female couple, considering how they'd seen male character Jack Harkness kiss the Doctor just half a season earlier[31].

The only possible reference to queer relationships is seen when Elton visits his childhood home and tells his audience that 'there's two women live there now and they're a bit severe, so never mind'. His pained face and the speed with which he moves on to a new topic aren't exactly beacons of queer representation. Still, this phrasing also echoes Davies' views on the hush-hush attitude towards queer people in less inclusive communities – how they may never explicitly be acknowledged as gay by their neighbours, but instead are seen simply as (to quote Davies) 'those two stern women who live together in that old house'[32].

Elton shows this attitude here, while he himself will go on to love someone in a way not accepted by society, which means there's a lot of dramatic irony hidden in his statement. Hidden very well, in fact, since without the knowledge that we're being asked to interpret Elton and Ursula as queer symbolism... the line just makes Elton

---

[31] *The Parting of the Ways* (2005).
[32] Davies, Russell T, and Benjamin Cook, *The Writer's Tale: The Final Chapter*, p592.

sound a bit awkward. All that might link Elton and Ursula to queerness is their first names. Elton mentions that he shares his name with gay pop star Elton John, and Ursula was most likely named for Ursula from Disney's *The Little Mermaid* (1989), a character with transformation powers who was in turn modelled after queer actor Divine. (Davies owns merchandise of the Disney character[33].) These links to queer culture are strained at best, and could be picked up on only by those already familiar with the topic.

More obviously than the queer symbolism, Ursula also becomes the sci-fi version of a disabled character. Davies names this as another intentional metaphor[34]. The sex lives of disabled people are sadly still considered taboo, both in fiction and in reality. An intimate relationship between a disabled character and an able-bodied one, as seen between Ursula and Elton, is a rare and precious thing in fiction indeed.

The choice to show ersatz versions of queer people and disabled people instead of the real thing can rightfully be criticised (see Chapter 7), but the intention is still admirable. We're invited to link Elton's identity and his outsider status to our own reality. Since we are both Elton's in-universe audience and **Doctor Who**'s actual audience, we have a chance to look at what we experience within the story, to take those experiences with us when we stop being Elton's one-off audience again, and to apply what we've learned to our everyday lives.

This storytelling style echoes not only Bertolt Brecht's structural

---

[33] Davies and Cook, *The Writer's Tale*, p394.
[34] **Toby Hadoke's Who's Round** #99.

alienation methods, but also decidedly similar sociopolitical goals. Namely, encouraging the spectators to change society for the better (i.e. to reflect on our own attitudes towards non-normative relationships), and to turn the gruesome losses that these figures suffer into positive life lessons for ourselves.

Brecht intentionally riled up theatregoers with barely-there sets, stilted dialogue, unnecessary plot twists and even direct insults across the fourth wall, hoping that his audiences would foster their resulting dissatisfaction and aim that anger at the social circumstances around them. A lofty plan – and one that more often than not failed, as most viewers got the dissatisfaction part down pat but then proceeded to simply go home and not change anything whatsoever. Similarly, if Davies' goal in writing *Love & Monsters* was to create dissatisfaction in **Doctor Who**'s audience in order to make them more empathetic about discrimination, the episode didn't convey those intentions as clearly as it could have.

But still, there's one obvious thing to be learned from *Love & Monsters*. 'When you're a kid,' Elton muses, 'they tell you it's all... Grow up. Get a job. Get married. Get a house. Have a kid, and that's it. But the truth is, the world is so much stranger than that. It's so much darker. And so much madder. And so much better.' What an amazing thing to hear. And this kind of encouragement can come across as patronising when spouted by a time traveller with a magic blue space box, but when it's Elton speaking to us from his bedroom, it rings true.

As Helbig describes in his narrative theory, a side character has playfully taken over the position of the expected lead characters, to interact with the audience in ways that the usual narrative would never allow[35]. And Elton's speech grows in meaning when we know what symbolism Davies was aiming for: in a world in which minorities encounter overwhelming resistance in finding work, expressing their love, being treated as equals on the housing market and raising children, these lines continue to be **gorgeously** uplifting.

The story's sex-positive attitude is emphasised with a rather cheeky allusion to oral sex, in its pre-watershed wording of having 'a bit of a love life'. That this love life is intended to be sexual is confirmed (albeit jokingly) by Davies: '[...] the thought of the Doctor walking in on Elton and Ursula's sex life could be rather marvellous. Poor Ursula. Or lucky Ursula.' In the same breath Davies also states that the two characters don't have unfinished business with the Doctor, indicating that they consider themselves complete just the way they are[36]. He claims that Ursula is an 'equal partner' in the relationship no matter her changed form[37].

This does leave us questioning, though, how a character cut off from all outside social interaction could be considered empowering or representative. Ursula becomes isolated to a much greater degree than disabled people in reality, due to the forced secrecy around her appearance. There's also the awkward question of how her relationship with Elton could ever be truly equal... on which more in Chapter 7.

The Role of Fannish Characters

LINDA can also be seen as intensely frustrating. The members are

---

[35] Helbig, *Intertextualität und Markierung*, p113.
[36] Davies and Cook, *The Writer's Tale*, p675.
[37] **Toby Hadoke's Who's Round** #99.

presented to us as symbolic fans, but as fans who know virtually nothing about the object of their obsession. They reflect our attempts to enjoy the world of **Doctor Who**, but their efforts go nowhere and end up killing most of them. Unlike Sally Sparrow, who takes over the Doctor's role for the duration of *Blink* and saves the TARDIS from the baddies, LINDA are barely a blip in the series' action. *Love & Monsters* treads a fine line between gently ribbing its audience – inviting us to have a bit of a chuckle at ourselves – and downright insulting us.

Director Dan Zeff claims that LINDA 'weren't people we were laughing **at**, they were people we were feeling **for**'[38]. But although creators can try to influence such a reception, they can't really demand it from their audience. It's up to us whether we see LINDA's obsession with the protagonists as a heartwarming wink and nod in our direction or as patronising and dismissive. When we're confronted with LINDA's lack of understanding of the Doctor, do we smile and say 'Oh, bless them!' or do we feel like the episode is holding up an embarrassing mirror to our faces? Do we treat LINDA the way we treat Rosencrantz and Guildenstern or **The Next Generation**'s lower deck crew – as loveable characters who just lack access to the full plot – or are Elton and his friends more likely to make us feel ashamed?

LINDA certainly aren't the first 'fan' characters to appear in **Doctor Who**. Several have appeared in the series over the years, ranging from sympathetic to comedic and from unsettling to downright villainous. There's a delicate balance between writing a fan character

---

[38] *Love & Monsters* DVD commentary, The Complete Second Series edition.

that the audience can identify with versus a fan character who's uncomfortably close to our most awkward moments. It's easy to tip the scale from writing a sympathetic fellow nerd lacking some social skills to including a cringeworthy figure whose entire existence mocks its audience. (Interestingly, Zeff insists that LINDA are not geeky[39], though that probably says more about the **Who** fan frame of reference than about the characters.)

One notorious fannish character is Whizz Kid in *The Greatest Show In The Galaxy* (1988-89), who – like LINDA – represents **Doctor Who**'s fanbase in none-too-flattering ways[40]. Much like LINDA, Whizz Kid wants to become part of the things he finds himself obsessed with, but lacks access to them. The character, while sweet, also comes across as admonishing to the viewers. Similar elements are seen in the portrayal of LINDA. Their obsessive over-analysing of the Doctor plus their stalking reflect the less savoury aspects of **Doctor Who**'s fandom. And like Whizz Kid, they end up dead as a result of their fannish glee.

A more recent fan-coded character in televised **Doctor Who** is Clive Finch in the episode *Rose*, who (like Ursula) runs a website about the Doctor. His role is to introduce the companion (and in the process the audience) to the Doctor's history. It's emblematic of Davies' era that even as a character who dies after he's fulfilled his narrative task, Clive is granted an on-screen family and a home. The

---

[39] *Love & Monsters* DVD commentary, The Complete Second Series edition.
[40] 'Fannish' here used not as an insult, but meaning 'relating to fans and fandom' as used in the academic field of fan studies and as a self-descriptor in fan communities.

combination of these elements – his fannish preoccupation with the Doctor and his visibly regular life – invites long-time fans of **Doctor Who** watching the first episode of the revival to identify with him. His subsequent death can be seen as a prelude to themes that would be explored in more depth with LINDA[41].

Two very endearing iterations of the 'fan of the Doctor' type are later seen in *Planet of the Dead*'s (2009) Malcolm and in the recurring character of Petronella Osgood, first appearing in *The Day of the Doctor* (2013). Their stories emphasise not just their obsessions with the Doctor but also their competence. Both are UNIT operatives who play key roles in keeping the Earth safe. Most importantly, both gain the friendly approval of the Doctor almost instantly, with Osgood (or possibly her Zygon double) even getting invited to see 'all of time and space' in *Death in Heaven* (2014). More complex fan-codings are additionally seen in the characters of Amy Pond and River Song.

While Elton eventually gets a sympathetic ear from the Doctor and Rose, this gesture comes after he's been solidly established as an outcast from the Doctor's world. And while the Doctor is willing to provide the man with closure, his opinion on Elton stays hidden to us. It wouldn't even be far-fetched to describe Elton as an antagonist. From having a door slammed shut on him by the Doctor in the opening sequence (a counterpoint to the familiar visual of a new companion walking through the TARDIS doors into the Doctor's life), to working for the villain and stalking the Tylers, and to finally being confronted by Rose for upsetting her mum, Elton is constantly seen

---

[41] For an in-depth look at Clive in relation to fandom, see Jon Arnold's **Black Archive** on *Rose*. Clive's life is additionally explored in detail in Davies' *Rose* Target novelisation.

in opposition to the TARDIS crew. This contrasts with the positive and helpful ways in which way Malcolm and Osgood are shown to be on the Doctor's side.

Fan Communities and the Search for Approval

LINDA's interpretive community sees its members sharing knowledge about the Doctor, and forming their opinions in dialogue with each other. The scenes in their basement hub show their mutual approval as they showcase their transformative works such as sculptures, character analyses and media presentations.

The way LINDA's members embody different aspects of fandom makes them recognisable. Each of them represents different aspects of fan engagement, whether social, affirmative (through data collection) or transformative (through creating fan works)[42].

Ursula is a photographer, site owner and event organiser, gathering the others around her to study the object of their interest. Elton is a video diarist and cover musician, full of enthusiasm, eager to be part of his obsession and to share it with the world. Bridget is an objective lore historian, presenting her meticulously gathered data and reconstructions to the group. Bliss is a fan artist, much less concerned with the reality of the Doctor and instead devoted to showing what he emotionally represents (using the alienating possibilities of making art to convey, in Shklovsky's terms, how things can be perceived rather than how they're already known[43]). And

---

[42] For extensive information on the topic, see Lamerichs, *Productive Fandom* as well as the Organization for Transformative Works' website and publications.
[43] Shklovsky, *Theory of Prose*, p6.

finally, Mr Skinner is a writer, inspired by the Doctor's mysteries to create his own suspenseful fiction. He also symbolises a fandom theorist or an academic fan, describing the Doctor in terms of archetypes – the **Fool**, the **Thief**, the **King**, the **Stranger**. Such words have often been used for the Doctor, both in and outside of the stories, and are recognisable for many long-time fans. 'The Stranger' in particular is the title of several unlicensed commercial works from the so-called 'Wilderness Years' between 1989 and 2005 when the franchise didn't exist in TV series format, starring thinly-veiled versions of the Doctor[44].

By providing symbolic commentary on the show that they themselves exist in, LINDA evoke the same methods that Brecht used in keeping his audiences critical. The layered storytelling, in which everything we see is filtered through Elton's narration, adds to this effect.

Similarly metatextual scenes are seen in Brecht's *Threepenny Opera*. The play's figures constantly enact make-believe scenes, personas and songs for each other, and afterwards evaluate each other's performances. A number of very similar sequences are seen in Stoppard's *Rosencrantz and Guildenstern Are Dead* and its film adaptation (each with different uses of this trope), as the titular characters interact with in-universe actors and become both spectators and accidental performers during in-universe plays.

---

[44] E.g. several BBV direct-to-video and audio releases titled **The Stranger** (1991-95) which starred sixth Doctor actor Colin Baker; as well as the pseudonymous Portia Da Costa's *The Stranger* (1997) in Virgin Books' **Black Lace** erotica range, featuring a barely disguised (and often just plain bare) eighth Doctor.

Brecht scholar Jan Knopf describes the effects of such a setup:

> 'Everything is staged; it's shown that things are being shown. At the same time, the audiences receive offers of judgment, because as the real-life viewers of the work of art they not only follow the various narratives within the narrative, but also receive cues from the performed audiences on the stage, through which the artistic expressions can be evaluated. As a result, they are directly asked to form an opinion for themselves, to criticise their own position as audiences, and to not in any way be enthralled or to "immerse" themselves in the characters.'[45]

Put more simply: when we see characters looking critically at art and at layers of narrative, this encourages us to also see the narrative from a critical point of view. When LINDA become audiences for each other's fanart and stories and theories, they continuously remind us of our own audience identity and our own fan reception. In particular, Elton's imitation of the Hoix ('it went RAAAWRGH!') echoes Brecht's performers-as-storytellers, who use their bodies to showcase past events while preventing the audience from getting too immersed. We're encouraged to be analytical in our interpretations by watching the characters being analytical and interpretive, and to be media-savvy by having the medium laid bare.

This effect is emphasised more than usual in *Love & Monsters*, but it can be seen throughout Davies' entire vision of **Doctor Who**. Talking about the structure of *Rose* as a template for his production style, he explains:

---

[45] Knopf, Jan, *Bertolt Brecht*, p119.

'When the Doctor blows up Henrik's, the explosion is reported on TV – and being commented on by Jackie, while her daughter was actually a witness. That's immediately, significantly, a new form of **Doctor Who**, because it's saying: this is public now. [...] That persisted, to become a spine of the entire series.'[46]

The Doctor's world is no longer isolated from everyday society. It's constantly in dialogue with it and its media, to be evaluated by the relatable in-universe public – which includes geeky little investigative groups like LINDA.

Fan communities revolving around shared hobbies can be especially tight-knit, as if its members speak a kind of shared, secret language with each other. Fan studies scholar Nicolle Lamerichs describes how fans 'interpret media experiences as an intense aesthetic experience that also differentiates them from others, both within the fan community and outside it. [...] In fandom, authors and readers engage in interpretive work and textual production together. Media fans have a shared lingua franca and social protocols' and fandom is 'a project of self-formation that is constantly enacted in fan practices'[47]. This process of developing an affinity space, an in-group, based on a shared interest is at the centre of *Love & Monsters*: Davies aims to 'dramatise the fun, honesty, support and friendships created by such groups'[48]. The playful nature of the group can be a nod to the metafictional game that Davies plays with us in this episode.

---

[46] Davies and Cook, *The Writer's Tale*, p701.
[47] Lamerichs, Nicolle, *Productive Fandom: Intermediality and Affective Reception in Fan Cultures*, p30.
[48] *The Complete History* #53, p53.

In his guide to literary theory, Brecht scholar Jürgen Schutte offers a summary of the three narrative levels we can spot here:

- The storytelling literary text is a poetic speech act, through which the **author** seeks to establish a **real communication** with an addressee / audience, at which his intention is aimed.
- The storytelling literary text constructs a **fictional communication situation** which is encapsulated by this poetic speech act, in which a **narrator** tells a story to a reader / listener.
- Within the storytelling literary text, a **fictional communication**, presented in various forms, takes place between **characters**.[49]

This means, in other (and less academically dense) words, that these three elements of *Love & Monsters* constantly strengthen each other:

- Davies lets us know that he's a fan just like we are.
- Elton lets us know that he's a fan just like we are.
- The LINDA members let each other know that they're all fans.

In showing us the happy side of fandom, Davies signifies that LINDA are a lot like we **Who** fans in all those sweet, productive ways – and that he sees himself as part of our fannish in-group.

The directorial and editing choices at this point of the episode emphasise harmony, happy music and emotional support. LINDA

---

[49] Schutte, *Einführung in die Literaturinterpretation*, p150. Emphasis in original.

create their own little nest of safety in their basement. It's a set intentionally chosen by Zeff as being too large for them, and styled with flaked paint and broken items to give 'a melancholy feel, an emptiness in the world around our characters'[50]. LINDA become the cohesion and warmth in this backdrop representation of a world that doesn't fit them. The Doctor as their common interest becomes just one of many things binding them together as they branch out into cooking, jamming, sharing original fiction, and even a little bit of romance.

Destructive Fans and Anoraks

It's therefore especially jarring when Victor Kennedy descends onto the community to become its leader. He interrupts LINDA's most overtly fannish group activity, a cover performance (of ELO's 'Don't Bring Me Down') with which they create their own version of existing music, to assert his own authority instead.

Where LINDA are meek and regular-looking, this villain is loud and appears especially refined. Where the group has spent its time gathering information about the Doctor bit by tiny bit, Kennedy waltzes in with extensive knowledge and a master plan. The contrast is clear. This is a man who uses fandom for his own goals. The fear of someone who can just barge in and completely overthrow the harmony of a small, close-knit group of nerds is, perhaps, even more real and immediate to viewers than any shop dummies or other

---

[50] **Doctor Who Confidential:** *The New World of Who* (2006). This is specified by the shooting script as well: 'Decaying, but not horribly so, just flaking plaster. Old chairs and desks piled up.' *The Complete History* #53, p54.

everyday objects **Doctor Who** turns into menaces.

Lamerichs defines productive fandom as something 'that borrows and repurposes existing cultural materials to produce something new'[51]. The Abzorbaloff craves the exact opposite. Instead of the way fans combine their enthusiasm with **borrowed** existing content to craft transformative works, he wants to combine the Doctor with himself – and destroy the Time Lord (and the fan community surrounding him) forever.

LINDA are obsessed, but they don't fully symbolise the 'wall of hostility'[52] that Davies has experienced from some fans. That role falls solidly to the Abzorbaloff. The monster personifies the showrunner's experiences with those 'angry, shrill voices who dominate the conversation'[53]. Elton's stalking of Jackie and Rose is also instigated by the villain's goals (although LINDA don't initially object). In his guise as Victor, the Abzorbaloff represents the truly obsessive fan – the kind that stalks, claims and devours. 'Just think about the Doctor,' he says as he explains his motivation. 'Oh, how will he taste? All that experience, all that knowledge.' His way of gaining said experience and knowledge is not to create fan works or to analyse the Time Lord's history, as LINDA has been doing, but to consume the Doctor whole. He wants to be the sole owner of the Doctor and the TARDIS – symbolically, of the entire mythos.

This is a realistic horror not only for the fanbase, but also specifically for the people involved in creating **Doctor Who**. 'It is', as sixth Doctor actor Colin Baker describes fans with destructive intentions, 'not an

---

[51] Lamerichs, *Productive Fandom*, p17.
[52] Davies and Cook, *The Writer's Tale*, p99.
[53] Davies and Cook, *The Writer's Tale*, p468.

unfamiliar position in fandom [...] to mistake being a fan of something to owning it.'[54] This dynamic between fans and creators echoes the same moral conflict that's at the core of the show: that of exploring the world versus ruling it.

At the same time, there's a temptation in the amount of knowledge that the Abzorbaloff offers LINDA. If the little group maps onto **Who** fandom, then the Abzorbaloff is also the kind of anorak who can provide taped stage shows, or out-of-print novels, or missing episodes unearthed from some dusty cupboard somewhere. He's the guy that a long-running show's creators turn to when they need a continuity advisor. As long as fans play nice and subject themselves to this type of person's abuse, they may just catch a glimpse of what they're chasing.

Davies writing an unrepentant villain as what he calls a 'super-fan'[55] leaves room for the more relaxed parts of the fanbase to identify with Elton and his friends, even when the episode pokes fun at them. Davies talks fondly about fans and fandom, refers to himself as part of these groups, praises people's extensive knowledge of **Doctor Who** and says that shame shouldn't ever enter into enjoying fandom and creating fan works[56]. He states that LINDA's fannishness is something for the viewers to enjoy rather than to feel bad about. *Love & Monsters* is 'absolutely'[57], as Davies assures us, a celebration

---

[54] Baker, Colin, 'I Was The Doctor And I'm Over The Moon That At Last We Have A Female Lead'.
[55] *The Complete History* #53, p53.
[56] **Toby Hadoke's Who's Round** #59, 'Russell T Davies: Part 3' and **Toby Hadoke's Who's Round** #99.
[57] **Toby Hadoke's Who's Round** #99.

of **Doctor Who** fandom:

> 'Because I can see so clearly, right in front of me, that the majority of fans are happy and fun and barmy, just like the show. And the most joyous thing of all is that every one of us [has] got a little blue box spinning somewhere in our heads. Spinning forever.'[58]

But considering its mixed reviews, it seems *Love & Monsters* didn't reach its viewer base the way it was intended to. Elton and the gang offer embarrassment where we expect escapism. The less flattering side of fandom depicted in this episode hit a nerve with viewers who felt themselves mocked and misrepresented. Not without reason, since this jokey portrayal of fans in media isn't an isolated incident. As fan studies scholar Lori Morimoto points out, there's a long history of content creators mocking their own fans in public spaces and even within the idolised works themselves. Morimoto describes quite bluntly how some creators see their fans: '[T]he problem – that is, what makes us so unworthy of serious consideration – is our emotional closeness to what we love.'[59]

Fans often explore their real-life circumstances by comparing their own identities to their favourite characters. Having this process

---

[58] Davies and Cook, *The Writer's Tale*, p468.
[59] Morimoto, Lori, 'Lecture 1: Acafandom and Ethics in Fan Studies'. For further reading, the following books offer some good entry points on fan representation in media: Jenkins, Henry, *Textual Poachers: Television Fans and Participatory Culture*; Larsen, Katherine and Lynn Zubernis, eds, *Fan Culture: Theory/Practice*; Bennett, Lucy and Paul Booth, eds, *Seeing Fans: Representations of Fandom in Media*; and Booth, Paul, *Playing Fans: Negotiating Fandom and Media in the Digital Age*.

suddenly imposed by the writers, in ways that link fan identity to meekness and to highly embarrassing fates, is not just uncomfortable but also downright invasive. There are definitely many more factors that led to criticism of the episode (see Chapters 5 and 7), but compared to the more flattering 'fan' portrayals such as Osgood in later **Doctor Who** stories, LINDA and the Abzorbaloff ended up receiving an unimpressed reception.

Still, however obnoxious, LINDA are a group of sweet, earnest and highly positive nerds. And it must be said – there are worse things for viewers to be represented as than a happy group of friends who lark about, eat cake together and sing ELO.

CHAPTER 3: 'THIS ISN'T, YOU KNOW, MY WHOLE LIFE'

Writing a New Main Character From Scratch

Love & Monsters started its life planned as a *Doctor Who Magazine* comic strip called 'I Love The Doctor'[60]. Davies envisioned a 'Clive-type internet-obsessed girl' stalker as his main character, observing 'her idol' and Rose through various adventures[61].

It was decided that the comic pitch would make a good TV episode instead. The female protagonist became a male one. The reason for this change, according to Davies, was that there had already been too many female characters who fancied the Doctor. He explains:

> 'Very soon after drawing this up, I looked at the amount of women in Series 2, especially those arguably in love with the 10th Doctor – Sarah Jane, Madame de Pompadour, not to mention Rose – and I decided that he'd broken too many female hearts! Time for a man! And so Elton was born.'[62]

Elton became platonically obsessed with the Doctor instead, seeking him out for more plot-heavy reasons than just a crush. (Why a male Elton couldn't be in love with the Doctor as well is unclear, but we should probably be grateful for this choice – a bloke obsessively stalking our male-presenting hero out of love/lust could have been awkward for queer representation.) This original draft concept of

---

[60] *The Complete History* #53, p50.
[61] Davies, Russell T, 'Second Sight', *Doctor Who Magazine* (DWM) Specials #14, *The Doctor Who Companion: Series Two*, p9.
[62] Davies, 'Second Sight', p9.

Elton saw the character witnessing events all the way back to the third Doctor's era, inspired by similar storytelling in the 1983 Woody Allen film *Zelig*[63].

This would have cemented him as a previously unnoticed pair of eyes not just in the lives of Rose and her Doctors but in the series as a whole. Elton would have been evacuated during *Remembrance of the Daleks* (1988), his mother would have been killed by a plastic daffodil controlled by the Nestene Consciousness during *Terror of the Autons* (1971) and he would have spotted the Loch Ness Monster in the Thames during *Terror of the Zygons* (1975)[64].

This idea was quickly discarded as being one step too far in terms of self-referential writing. Although it might have enabled fans of 20th-century **Doctor Who** to recognise their own memories more easily in the character, the idea would have alienated pretty much everyone else. But it would have been an admirable example of what fandoms call 'fanwank' – a term coined by **Who** novelist Craig Hinton to describe his own writing style – meaning excessive exposition which adds detail to unrelated stories.

Critic John Seavey explains: 'When a writer writes in a monologue that explains what happened to the second Zygon fleet, in a novel that features no Zygons, that's fanwank.' The practice is:

> 'a sort of Grand Design for the **Doctor Who** universe, filled with explanations of how the different dimensions and the Time Vortex and the various cosmic entities we've seen over the years interacted. It makes sense, it forms a self-consistent

---

[63] *The Complete History* #53, p50.
[64] *Love & Monsters* DVD commentary.

whole... but I don't think it was ever particularly wanted or needed.'[65]

Seavey's statement is a subjective one, of course. Plenty of writers embrace such things wholeheartedly and write them into their stories on purpose. The expectation of gratuitous references has become an ingrained part of the franchise which the writers constantly have to navigate in their plotting.

In any case, with this fanwanky draft concept Davies (and in a sense Elton himself) would have demonstrated what **Doctor Who**'s fan-creators do best. As literary scholar Balaka Basu beautifully describes it, 'they fill in interstitial gaps and unanswered questions in already extant narratives, they mimic style, and using bricolage, they create new texts within previously defined parameters.'[66] This effect persists in the final script by having Elton experience events of *Rose* and *Aliens of London*, albeit in a way that's more accessible to the revival's brand new audience. The footage of the Doctor and Rose presented by the Abzorbaloff also avoids any overly nostalgic self-referencing. We have a chance to see Elton and the rest of LINDA being part of the regular contemporary world, without them having to be overly rooted in **Doctor Who** itself.

The Elton we ended up with is decidedly streamlined. This is true not only for his backstory and behaviour, but also for his appearance. The

---

[65] Seavey, John, 'Craig Hinton'.
[66] Basu, Balaka, 'When Worlds Continue: The Doctor's Adventures in Fandom and Metatextuality' in Hansen, Christopher J, ed, *Ruminations, Peregrinations, and Regenerations: A Critical Approach to **Doctor Who***, p170.

script specifies him as having 'no funny voice or daft clothes'[67]. Warren's take on Elton is restrained as well – interestingly so, since his acting in *Terry Pratchett's Hogfather* (2006) proved that his capacity for ham knows no bounds. And most references to Elton's daily life outside of LINDA and ELO ended up being cut from the final broadcast version, including the entire existence of his landlady[68].

But the result of this streamlining is also that, although he assures us that this isn't his whole life, we have little else to go on in defining him. Elton is a stripped-down person, appearing to us only with those aspects of his life that are relevant to us as viewers. It could be said that Elton's life outside of what we see is somewhat of a void, an empty space to be filled in by our own imaginations. Although his personality is pretty defined, his everyday life (or lack thereof) allows us to project our own circumstances onto him. Whether this makes him easier or harder to identify with is a question to which, I think, there are as many answers as there are viewers.

The City of Lost Nerds

The normalcy of LINDA's point of view is underlined with a completely Earthbound backdrop. Gone are the glitz and glamour of the sci-fi genre, gone are the alien worlds and breath-taking starscape effects. The episode's placement makes this change especially stand out, coming right after *The Impossible Planet / The Satan Pit*, which featured the first properly alien (i.e. not a copy of Earth) planet in Davies' **Doctor Who**.

Elton's bedroom is described in the script as 'nice, simple, not jokey

---

[67] *The Complete History* #53, p54.
[68] *The Complete History* #53, p63.

or cluttered'[69]. It's cosy and a little luxurious, with its slanted ceiling and foofy cushions, but still as normal as they come. The items around him include glass bottles, books, potted plants, some wall decals and football merchandise. The room offers no further clues about his interests outside of LINDA, and where other stories may have been tempted to include Easter egg nods to specific bits of pop culture, *Love & Monsters* seems to avoid this deliberately. The everyman blankness of Elton's room may be interpreted as an invitation to identify more with him, to fill in those blanks for ourselves. But seeing as we're watching a sci-fi programme and can therefore be presumed to be on the geeky side, the occasional space poster or nerdy mug decal might have helped.

The location shooting takes us to anonymous, everyday Cardiff streets. We're told these places represent London, but they could be found almost anywhere in the United Kingdom (and quite a way beyond). The normalcy of this backdrop is another opportunity to relate more strongly to LINDA. It stands in contrast to the London landmarks featured, for example, in *Rose* and *The Bells of Saint John* (2013). While none of us could realistically fight aliens under the London Eye or ride a motorcycle up the Shard, most people are quite capable of sitting on park benches, going for a city stroll or navigating gentle slopes. This mundanity can showcase **Doctor Who** plots next to everyday experiences. The Tylers' estate uses this effect to bring the Doctor into 'our' home in the 2005 season; *Love & Monsters*, conversely, uses it to show how far away we as regular humans actually are from the Doctor's world.

The outside scenes are also noticeably abandoned (read:

---

[69] *The Complete History* #53, p54.

wonderfully cheap to cast). There are practically no passers-by, shops, pets, or any other kinds of **life** seen for much of the story. As a result, LINDA come across as abandoned as well, navigating a gloomy void around them and becoming all the more strongly coded as outcasts in the process. Zeff and his design team deliberately emphasised 'big urban spaces that once may have been full of life, but now lay abandoned, rusting, decayed. Amidst this, Elton and his fragile group of friends would almost feel cast adrift – increasingly vulnerable as they are led astray by the sinister Victor Kennedy.'[70]

This aesthetic can be felt throughout the episode. The outside scenes are dirty, cold and filled with skeletal construction work. One shooting location, still a derelict area in the episode's planning stages, was even dropped at the last moment because it had started to look too modern and in use[71]. It's an old storytelling technique, and one that was also praised by Brecht and Skhlovsky: to contrast meaningful emotional experiences with the automatisation of an industrialised lifestyle. In classic alienation theories, the imagery of an anonymised cityscape that's visibly being constructed, but of which the creation process is inaccessible to our heroes, served to illustrate alienation from industrial production methods and from familiar societal rules. For LINDA, this backdrop means alienation from **everything**... including from their own favourite alien.

It isn't until Elton seeks out Jackie that the world around him changes again – taking him into a bustling marketplace, a busy launderette and all the other everyday aspects of Jackie's warm, motherly world.

---

[70] *The New World of Who*.
[71] *The Complete History* #53, p56ff.

The Unreliable Narrator

Because we become Elton's camcorder audience, it's unclear how we're also seeing the events outside of the camera perspective. He tells is 'it's not just me sitting here talking' but to his in-universe viewers, it would actually be mostly that. The only camcorder footage not shot in his bedroom (near Elton's childhood home, filmed by Ursula before her transformation) immediately follows this scene and doesn't show us anything substantial. So do we see the sci-fi adventure the same way we see any other **Doctor Who** story? Or are we, as his in-universe camcorder audience, imagining the story guided by his narration? Meaning: do we treat the episode's visuals as 'true' or as a potential fiction within the fiction?

To Davies, the video diary format means 'not being limited to a straightforward telling' of his story[72]. Aside from the obvious, chronological meaning of straightforward, we can also ask: is Elton straightforwardly honest with us? Should we trust his narration?

The Hoix chase at the start of the narrative is an exaggerated comedy bit, referencing classic stage plays, films and cartoons in which characters would chase each other through long corridors with doors on either side. The chase in *Love & Monsters* sees the Doctor and Rose seemingly teleporting from one side of the corridor to another. It's an over-the-top send-up of all that running through corridors that **Doctor Who** is famous for. Of course, an actual teleporter might be hiding just off-screen; this being **Who**, nothing could be so impossible that it would definitively indicate unreliable narration or break our immersion in the fiction. Whatever the case, even though

---

[72] Davies and Cook, *The Writer's Tale*, p34.

we may accept that this actually happened to the Doctor and Rose, it's still such an obvious parody that it casts doubt on Elton's storytelling.

The hazy, distorted childhood memories Elton has of the Doctor also form part of his unreliability. But these additionally map onto his fan identity: just like viewers of **Doctor Who** have to rely on childhood memories, fan reconstructions and altered texts in order to experience the junked episodes of the Doctor's earliest adventures, Elton tries to understand what happened by re-interpreting his memory of the Doctor in a fan community setting. If the Abzorbaloff stands in for the kind of super-fan who could provide such missing chunks of lore to the fandom in their original form, Elton's willingness to put up with him suddenly makes a lot more sense. Because even though Elton's own storytelling may not always accurately reflect what happened, his ultimate goal is to find clarity and truth.

Throughout the episode, there are other scenes that show Elton's narration as unreliable: his improbably exploding computer, his talk of inventing a 'pulley system' to reach his shoes. The most playful demonstration of this takes place during his first time meeting Jackie:

ELTON [OC]

Step four, find some subtle way to integrate yourself into the target's household.

JACKIE

Mind you, I'm only down here because my washing machine's knackered. I don't suppose you're any good at fixing things, are you?

While Elton is monologuing about subtle infiltration, Jackie is actually the one to start the conversation and invite him over. In this launderette sequence, we're allowed to instantly **see** that his narration doesn't line up with what happened. This means that either we're objective onlookers here who can see and hear things as they actually went down, or that the discrepancy between Elton's narration and the actual events is a cheeky, deliberate joke on his part. Does he determine what we see here, much like he decides the narrative chronology for us? Or can we go behind his back (so to speak) and see what truly happened, from a neutral point of view beyond his control? Either way, we're left disoriented and with little seeds of suspicion planted in our minds.

This unreliable narration also reminds us that regardless of how many layers of narrative we're in, everything we're being shown is a deliberately constructed work of fiction that should be treated critically. Davies invokes his own view of television production as a process that should be transparent, demystified and democratised. Echoing Brecht's views practically to the letter, Davies states that by giving audiences direct insight into the creation of a show, he means for them to stay aware of the **artificiality** of it all, and to know that they too can become part of the behind-the-scenes efforts that go into creating a narrative[73].

Elton's own camera is a symbol of this attitude. The same goes for the launderette sequence, which highlights the fictionality (and in a Brechtian sense, the unreliability and **changeability**) of everything we're shown. Maybe even the skeletal and half-constructed

---

[73] Russell, Gary, **Doctor Who**: *The Inside Story – The Official Guide to Series 1 and 2*, p254.

buildings in the episode are part of the same authorial intention – these can symbolise alienation for LINDA, but like Brecht's dingy cardboard sets they can also provide a sense of transparency, of the story as a work in progress that requires the audience's participation in its construction. In any case, the story's setup keeps us aware of our double identity as Elton's in-universe audience and as our real-life selves.

In the final scene, these little seeds of doubt open up another possibility. When we see Ursula's transformed body, we do so by breaking away from the camcorder point of view and going back to the spatial position we usually have as **Doctor Who** viewers. The 'neutral' device of the camcorder never lets us see what's on the slab. We may therefore choose to believe that Ursula's new form exists in Elton's imagination and narration alone. Maybe we as in-universe camcorder viewers are only **imagining** her face, based on what he wants us to think; or maybe we're even seeing directly into his head.

This would make our spatial positions outside of the camcorder recordings an **additional** fictional state, on top of our assumed identity as the in-story audience. This theory has some holes in it (after all, we also hear Ursula speaking while we're still within the camcorder perspective) but has nonetheless gained traction in fandom. As Jon Arnold asks: 'How many other *Doctor Who* episodes have the courage to provide you with an opportunity to disregard them if you don't like them?'[74]

Even Davies' Target novelisation of *Rose* leaves Elton out of events

---

[74] Arnold, 'Love & Monsters', p104.

which he claims to have been present for, despite the book featuring cameos of several other incidental characters, including Donna Noble. Is Davies still emphasising Elton's marginalisation from the overall story of **Doctor Who** here, or is he implying that Elton's actually a fantasist who wasn't there at all?

Unreliable narrators and contradictory story elements are found all over Brecht's works as well. The anonymous narrative voice of the *Threepenny Novel*, specifically, is blatantly contrasted with the story itself. For example, when Fewkoombey starts to earn a living as a beggar after long periods of distress, the narration tells us with disturbing calmness of his 'luck'[75]. Brecht used this method to keep his readers critical. Even when Brecht's narrators present us their world directly through the eyes of the figures, their words are still unreliable, to indicate that **all** aspects of society are artificially constructed through other people's questionable agendas.

By emphasising that even the voices guiding us through the stories couldn't be trusted, the playwright encouraged his fans to keep thinking for themselves instead of getting immersed, and to question everything both inside and outside of the fiction. He wanted to give spectators a sense of helpless frustration, by not providing answers; followed by a strong sense of agency, as the viewers themselves start piecing possible answers together using their own frames of reference. This was meant to remind viewers of how they may sometimes feel helpless in daily life, followed by the realisation that this helplessness can be overcome. When social dynamics are presented as contradictory, this means that they can also be contradict**ed**, questioned and changed. In Brecht's narrative style

---

[75] Brecht, Bertolt, *Threepenny Novel*, p10.

there's no objectively 'true' version of a tale which audiences can **re**-construct just by observing – but rather an intentionally disjointed collection of elements, from which each individual spectator is invited to construct something new[76]. This storytelling technique acknowledges and encourages the fannish power to create meaning from the materials provided by each text.

So let's apply that mindset here and question what we're seeing. Davies makes us think about the frustration of being gay in a heteronormative world, or disabled in an ableist society, and we can become actively compassionate about these things as a result. Elton and Ursula are the unreliable catalysts of this process. Their ending can be a reason for us to think critically, because it leaves us with a whole lot of questions left unanswered.

Let's suppose that Elton isn't actually holding Ursula's new body. What does that say about him? Does it present him as someone with an overactive imagination, or as someone who's literally hallucinating Ursula's transformation? After all, it's odd how he talks about her in the past tense: 'She was like a proper mate. Poor Ursula...'

Taking it one step further, we can choose to believe that even the in-universe audio and camera visuals are unreliable (a line of critical thinking also specifically encouraged by Brecht). This would explain how Ursula's voice is heard in the recording before we cut to a point of view by Elton's side. As in Brecht's works, it could be a signal that even we, whether in our in-universe guise as Elton's voyeuristic

---

[76] Explored in Barnett, *Brecht in Practice*, p40ff and passim throughout the book.

audience or simply as ourselves, are unreliable in the way we interpret things. It could mean that we must therefore constantly question our own perception – both in watching **Doctor Who** and on a larger, real-life scale. On top of that, why should we assume that Elton's camera recordings actually attract an in-universe audience? Could he just be rambling away to his camcorder without a viewer base, convincing himself that someone, one day, will want to watch his stories? Is he himself a creator without a fandom? Are we, the real-life viewers, his ersatz fandom **because** no one in-universe will see him?

Could Elton's delusions even be the direct result of the Doctor's actions, leaving him traumatised to the point of psychological breakdown? As critic Alasdair Wilkins points out, this ambiguity causes the episode to zig-zag Elton's character to a potentially detrimental degree. 'It's not that a man with possibly serious mental health issues is incapable of such understanding and perception;' Wilkins states, 'indeed, that would be a fine point for **Doctor Who** to get across. But the varying portrayals of Elton never quite gel together to make such an interpretation feel earned.'[77]

With all these explanations to choose from, it seems there are as many possible Eltons and Ursulas as there are viewers. And so, as the credits roll and we leave Elton behind again, we can't be altogether sure what we've just witnessed. All we know is that on some level... we've been taken for a ride.

---

[77] Wilkins, Alasdair, '**Doctor Who**: *Love & Monsters / Fear Her*'.

CHAPTER 4: 'GREAT BIG ABSORBING CREATURE FROM OUTER SPACE'
What Rough Beast

Let's get the obvious out of the way: the Abzorbaloff is silly. He's a farting mess of flabby skin on legs, chasing Elton through an everyday neighbourhood in broad daylight, his tongue hanging out and everything.

Of course, there are ways in which that sort of thing can work. A disgusting baddie can be as scary as a refined one. A villain in broad daylight can be as effective as one lurking in the shadows. And as for normal city backgrounds – bringing a monster close to the viewers' own surroundings can make it feel more immediate and therefore more threatening. Like third Doctor actor Jon Pertwee was fond of saying, there's nothing more scary than coming home to find 'a Yeti on your loo in Tooting Bec'[78]. Davies agrees: 'The ordinary turned into the extraordinary. That's very **Doctor Who**. Turning suburbia into terror.'[79]

What Pertwee didn't mention there is that an actor in a rubber suit walking around in everyday scenery is also really easy on production. This was certainly a factor in the Abzorbaloff's development. The episode was conceived by Davies to require only a few CGI effects, as it would be filmed towards the end of the recording slate, leaving FX studio The Mill relatively little time to complete the digital frames. A humanoid baddie allowed for many practical effects, which took

---

[78] 'Introduction to *The Web of Fear*'.
[79] Davies and Cook, *The Writer's Tale*, p33.

pressure off both the budget and the production schedule. The series breakdown had Davies describe the monster with: 'whatever it is, it should be a practical build, not CGI'[80]. The final product did include more CGI shots than planned, due to the animatronic faces on the Abzorbaloff looking a bit too animatronic[81], but the amount of digital work was still low compared to other episodes.

The villain ended up being brought to life by the popular Bolton comedian Peter Kay. A long-time fan of the series, Kay had previously sent Davies a six-page handwritten letter gushing about **Doctor Who**'s revival, and asking to play a character on the show[82]. He was offered the part of Elton but opted to play the Abzorbaloff instead[83]. Kay worked closely with Davies to develop the character, even inviting himself into the showrunner's house to discuss his scenes[84]. And Kay's face-cast was already in the Millennium FX database from having starred in BBC's **The Catherine Tate Show** (2004-07), which allowed for his mask to be fitted cheaply and with little fuss[85].

With all that background knowledge, though, what we have is still fundamentally a silly beastie doing silly things. Even if placed in a more serious episode, the Abzorbaloff would hardly be the most intimidating monster in **Doctor Who**'s rogues' gallery. He is, to quote

---

[80] Davies, 'Second Sight', p9.
[81] *Love & Monsters* DVD commentary, The Complete Second Series edition.
[82] *The Complete History* #53, p51.
[83] *The Complete History* #53, p53.
[84] *Love & Monsters* DVD commentary.
[85] *The Complete History* #53, p58.

Zeff, 'just a bloke from his planet'[86]. But we can take a moment to look beyond the flapping rubber and see what else the Abzorbaloff can represent.

The Road to Power

The script describes Kennedy wearing an 'expensive coat, felt collar, like he imagines himself as a gangster. In one hand, an expensive briefcase, in the other – at all times – a silver-topped cane'[87].

Davies couldn't have echoed Brecht more strongly if he'd tried. The gangster villain of Brecht's *Threepenny Opera* and *Threepenny Novel*, Mack the Knife, went about in the same pompous style. This way, the figure of Mack was intended to evoke the robber baron of anti-capitalist / Marxist discourse – the untouchable criminal, symbolic of structural class imperatives, who gets away with oppression by invoking his authority and wealth. In a larger sense, Mack symbolised Brecht's idea of capitalism itself.

This fascist, authoritarian baddie embodies, to quote Brecht,

> 'a bourgeois appearance. The preference of the bourgeoisie for robbers is explained by a misconception: namely, that a robber is not a bourgeois. This misconception has as its parent another misconception: namely, that a bourgeois is not a robber.'[88]

By presenting Mack as a criminal but also with all the affected pomp

---

[86] *Love & Monsters* DVD commentary, The Complete Second Series edition.
[87] *The Complete History* #53, p54.
[88] Brecht, Bertolt, 'Anmerkungen zur *Dreigroschenoper*' ['Notes on the "Threepenny Opera"'] in *Schriften 4*, p60.

and power of the bourgeoisie, Brecht used Marxist aesthetics to say that those in power can also be everyday villains. He invited his audiences to conflate vulgar criminals and the ruling classes, and he offered Mack's posh looks as a clear visual cue.

It would probably be silly to assume that Davies secretly served up Marxist discourse with this episode. None of the parallels between *Love & Monsters* and Brecht's works seem to be deliberate. Still, let's examine the Abzorbaloff a bit more in this context. His clothes invoke wealth and power; his silver cane is aristocratic grandeur. His fake name, Victor Kennedy, scans as 'Conqueror President'. The prequel short ('Tardisode 10') sees Kennedy sitting at a posh desk in a large, CEO-like room and having his own private secretary. Even his way of speaking is overly cultured, and turns out to be affected when the disguise is dropped and Kay's native Bolton takes its place[89]. This is a textbook Brechtian contradiction, in which class is presented as just another social construct.

But the words 'imagines himself as a gangster' in Davies' script are key here. Like the Abzorbaloff, Brecht's gangster figure draws on his authoritative appearance to control his lackeys. He exaggerates his cultivated reputation of being a dangerous, powerful man (hence that catchy song about Mack's supposed crimes) in order to stay in charge. He gains power over others by presenting himself as having power over others. And so he becomes what he imagines himself to be, by making others see him that way, using his reputation as a tool. For Brecht, this narrative technique was pure Marxism – he wrote his stories to expose what he saw as the undeserved authority of the bourgeoisie, and the ways their façades of power help them stay in

---

[89] As decided by Kay and Davies. *Love & Monsters* DVD commentary.

power.

Whether or not Davies intended it, we can see these views echoed in *Love & Monsters* as well. The Abzorbaloff shows how community-based fannish devotion is vulnerable to enclosure, commodification and absorption by those who stand to gain from it. The dynamic between LINDA and the Abzorbaloff symbolises a world in which, to quote critic Jack Graham, 'all human enthusiasms and capacities are slaved to a maniacally ravenous, pinstriped monster of consumption'[90]. LINDA's private production of fan works is stripped of its affective use value (what things can be used for) by the Abzorbaloff and transformed into working for exchange value (what things can be traded for) instead[91]. That which Marx considered an inhuman form of labour, the alienation of the worker from the value of their work, is imposed here by a literal alien.

Doctor Who has always mocked the overly rich and powerful, such as the aristocratic Time Lords that the Doctor ran away from in the first place – those who fancy themselves the ruling class of all of time and space. But in *Love & Monsters'* homage to fans, the Abzorbaloff wasn't intended to symbolise those actually ruling over the fandom. He's instead designed to embody those fans who, like Mack the Knife, use their own reputations and accomplishments to make themselves **seem** powerful and in charge. The monster represents those super-fans who think their status should give them the power to control their fellow geeks, the fan culture, and the canon itself[92].

---

[90] Graham, Jack, 'Love & People'.
[91] For a detailed criticism of use value / exchange value discourse and cultural capital in relation to fandom, see Hills, Matt, *Fan Cultures*.
[92] *The Complete History* #53, p53.

Here we reach an interesting bit of Marxist discourse in relation to the episode. Because in **Doctor Who**, nearly everyone who's now in charge was once just another super-fan. What is Davies, if not a fan who made his way through the BBC ranks using his reputation's exchange value? Has he not, as broadcast media historian Douglas McNaughton puts it, 'converted his fan cultural capital into institutional power through his television writing career'[93] to gain control? What did he do but take the reins of canon and become its ruler? Is he not, in some sense, the robber baron of the show – the arbiter of continuity, absorbing story ideas left and right from the Wilderness Years' audios and books to regurgitate them on our screens? Even when he tells us that it's an 'idiot equation' to treat only the TV stories as canon[94], has he not taken control of the very definition of **Doctor Who** in public consciousness?

But (I hear you cry) wasn't Davies also part of the poor masses? One of us? A simple worker who (as some might put it) escaped his life as a mechanistic cog of fan reception and, through revolutionary thinking, secured the means of production to distribute **Who** back among the crowd?

The answer of course is that he's both. Much as the robber baron figure can reach his status through genuine passion for his work, much as socioeconomic changes and shifting class structures can propel people from the proletariat to the ruling classes, **Doctor**

---

[93] McNaughton, Douglas, 'Regeneration of a Brand: The Fan Audience and the 2005 **Doctor Who** Revival' in *Ruminations, Peregrinations, and Regenerations*, p197.
[94] Cook, Benjamin, *Doctor Who: The New Audio Adventures: The Inside Story*, p.3.

Who's showrunner can be both a loving fanboy and the walking embodiment of ownership. The show was brought back by the fans and for the fans – but there's a constant discrepancy in its control lying in the hands of the few, while it's **simultaneously** said to belong to the fandom as a whole.

In the end, this will have played a part in the episode's reception. Where Davies may see himself as just another fan having a laugh at super-fans by our side, we're aware that he holds more power, and stands at a greater distance from us, than any annoying old super-fan we meet in our own LINDA-like community circles. The Abzorbaloffs who barge into our areas of fandom may be loud, and may spoil the fun a little – but few of them can truly upset the show or establish the continuities like Davies can. As showrunner, he holds all the power over **Doctor Who** that the Abzorbaloff symbolically hungers for.

Davies isn't in LINDA anymore, no matter how much he assures us that he's a fan just like the rest of us. He's left that world for good. And because most of us are on LINDA's level of fandom, the effect of the episode isn't only that of a fan joining his fellow fans for a round of gentle ribbing. It's also that of a member of the ruling classes slumming it. And, well... no one likes to be reminded that they're stuck in the proverbial slums.

Mythical Convictions

These means of production look somewhat different in **Doctor Who** than they do in most other franchises, though. There are several reasons for this:

- **Doctor Who** is an unusually long-running and

collaborative fiction, with many of its creators themselves being fans, their own production often having started out like the fan-coded creative activities seen in LINDA.
- There is no singular copyright holder for all elements of the franchise. Even the copyright of something as integral as the Daleks isn't clear-cut, and has led to heated legal battles[95].
- Spinoffs and tie-ins can spiral out into franchises of their own, using the intellectual property of those fan-creators who originated their own lore elements, often without requiring permission from **Doctor Who**'s owners.
- Lore elements from the TV series, spinoffs, tie-ins and other media can mutually influence each other, regardless of which licences (if any) these stories have.
- Since multiple timelines, universes and paradoxes exist within **Doctor Who**, no creator has the power to claim a true canon or to invalidate the works of any other.

These factors impact the way 'canon' is treated in **Doctor Who**, and strongly affect the socioeconomic relationships between product owners and fan-creators.

(At this point, I should emphasise that socioeconomic theories deal with people's actual access to basic human needs. While it's fun to draw comparisons between Marxism – or any other socioeconomic discourse – and the creation of a silly TV show, this can't reflect the scope of such issues. This book isn't in any way intended to dismiss

---

[95] 'BBC wins battle over Dalek book'.

people's lived experiences, and it's important to remember the dangers of entitlement in thinking about luxury goods and services in terms of redistribution. With that said...)

The collaborative process of **Doctor Who**'s creation is part of a growing global trend. People who create fan works, as LINDA are shown to do, are becoming increasingly influential within popular culture. This shift was made possible by the skyrocketing global interconnectedness of niche communities and the ease with which fans can now find like-minded people online via websites much like Ursula's. The road from fan artist, fanfic writer or fandom analyst to professional geek can be a pretty smooth one these days. To quote Lori Morimoto, participatory fan cultures just like LINDA thrive by fans 'poaching the characters, sometimes the tropes [...] to write what they wanted to see' in response to existing works[96].

Such 'poaching' is a way for fans to question and subvert the power that franchise owners assert, and to claim the means of cultural production for themselves. Fan studies pioneer Henry Jenkins emphasises how the creation of fan works challenges 'the authority which readers grant to textual producers'[97]. 'Fans', he writes, 'reject

---

[96] Morimoto, 'Lecture 1'.
[97] Jenkins, *Textual Poachers*, p78. For further reading, Jenkins points (albeit a bit sceptically) to historian Michel de Certeau, who coined the term 'poaching' for transformative works in his book *The Practice of Everyday Life*. The dynamic between fan-creators and franchise owners is also explored extensively in Jenkins' books *Convergence Culture* and *Science Fiction Audiences: Watching Star Trek and Doctor Who* (co-written with John Tulloch) as well as in Mark Deuze's *Media Work*. Jenkins recommends Mark Andrejevic's essay 'Watching

the idea of a definitive version produced, authorized, and regulated by some media conglomerate. Instead, fans envision a world where all of us can participate in the creation and circulation of central cultural myths.' The 'right to participate in the culture' is a 'freedom' which fans claim for themselves. It is emphatically not a privilege granted by the rich. Nor is it something fans are 'prepared to barter away for better sound files' or other resources, which franchise owners sometimes provide to fan projects to be used exclusively on their own strict terms[98].

When LINDA sell themselves out for the Abzorbaloff's crisp footage and grand plans, this villain parallels both the overbearing super-fans who might bring in missing episodes and the media conglomerates who try to guard their copyright and to control fannish works. It's fitting that they eventually tear him apart. Fan groups can stand up to the real-life Abzorbaloffs who try to assert power over the fandom, to those who allow creative access to the media only in exchange for obedience. By acknowledging the transformative power of fans like LINDA, *Love & Monsters* presents the canonical authority of those in charge not as something mythical and untouchable, but simply as part of a constantly evolving and **changeable** dialogue.

'Fan culture', Jenkins states, 'stands as an open challenge to the "naturalness" and desirability of dominant cultural hierarchies,' being a 'refusal of authorial authority and a violation of intellectual

---

Television Without Pity: The Productivity of Online Fans' for a balanced socioeconomic counterpoint to his own perspectives.
[98] Jenkins, Henry, *Convergence Culture*, p256.

property.'[99] This dominance and this intellectual property are ideas which the Abzorbaloff can symbolise in his attempts to control and to appropriate LINDA's fan works. He tries to turn his position as leader of a fan group into a new role as someone who would contain all the Doctor's knowledge and power inside himself, denying access to anyone else. That is, he tries to become the Doctor's owner, as a real-life fan might try to become **Doctor Who**'s owner.

In destroying the monster, Elton and his friends show the power of fans to reject that kind of authority, and defiantly to create and defend their own collaborative spaces. The fact that Davies himself is a super-fan who made it to the top, who seems to have gained all the power which the Abzorbaloff wants, adds some delicious narrative irony to this sequence.

Of Canonicity and Likelihood

Drawing on the ideas put forth by Jenkins, Morimoto explains that the transformation of existing media through, for example, fanfiction and fanart is one of the factors that have gradually made fans the creators of popular culture in recent years, rather than just of counterculture. This revolutionary process was made possible, she says, because 'poaching was understood as something that could undermine mass media messages, and this was what made it worth our consideration'. By being more daring, more community-oriented and more openly political than the source material, geeky works that transformed existing stories became a huge part of the new mass media, replacing the old mass media. Or to put it bluntly, fan works

---

[99] Jenkins, *Textual Poachers*, p72.

'fought the man'[100].

Fans have many roads to creating **Doctor Who** material and turning their poaching into gamekeeping. They can become part of the series' production through conventional TV careers, or thrive in the show's tie-ins and spinoffs. Many of the stories outside of the TV series and/or the **Who** brand indeed fight 'the man' (or in Mary Whitehouse's case, the woman): they've continuously contributed new aspects to the lore by being more irreverent, more adult and more queer than what the BBC allowed at the time.

Unlike franchises which have a rigid boundary between core canon and apocryphal works, **Doctor Who**'s mythos is quite fluid. Stories can end up patchworks of mutually contradictory elements, introduced in wildly different media over the years by wildly different copyright holders. The TV series is not necessarily the core text for every fan: McNaughton states that 'before time-shifting technology such as video-recording, many fans experienced **Who** not only, or even primarily, as television, but through other media, building into a complex meta-text.'[101] This holds even more true in our multimedial online culture nowadays.

Additionally, the franchise is not cordoned off: some writers introduce their own previously published characters into **Doctor Who** stories, or transfer their **Who** characters into fiction that doesn't explicitly carry the **Who** brand. These in turn can have their own spinoffs and tie-ins, which retain the narrative links to be seen as part of **Who** lore and the power to influence the overarching

---

[100] Morimoto, 'Lecture 1'.
[101] McNaughton, 'Regeneration of a Brand', p195.

mythos regardless of their licensing.

Such a structure raises questions about what it means to view **Who**'s constantly unfolding tale through the lens of 'core canon' versus 'expanded universe' – that is, as a matter of the top versus the slums. In fact, McNaughton is far from alone in his opinion that when Davies was writing for Virgin Books' **New Adventures** range of novels while the show was off the air, he was already creating the at-the-time most official and therefore main canonical version of **Doctor Who**[102]. Others dismiss such works as fannish and non-canonical, preferring to see only the TV series as 'real'. Every fan decides for themself which stories they consider valid. The franchise never truly had a traditional tree structure, with the TV series being the trunk and all other works branching out from there only with the Executive Producers' permission. Instead, it's much more like a universe-sized arras in which all the threads overlap and braid together.

Bliss' art, Elton's vlogs and cover songs, Bridget's research, Ursula's website curating and Mr Skinner's writing are examples of the kinds of fan output which can become part of **Who**'s sprawling lore over time. The power that we personally determine fan productions to have in our enjoyment of **Doctor Who** may therefore directly influence whether we see fan-coded characters like LINDA as ineffectual or as capable; as separate from the Doctor's life or as profoundly interwoven with it.

The Unanchored Thread of Time

Doctor Who lore is, as writer Alex Marchon puts it, like a proper history 'in that it's a collection of vastly different accounts of events

---

[102] McNaughton, 'Regeneration of a Brand', p196.

from vastly different viewpoints written with vastly different agendas in mind'[103]. In fact, we can go one step further: unlike real-life history, the franchise doesn't even have a singular, rigidly objective timeline to cling to. Time in **Doctor Who** can evolve, branch off and form stable paradoxes. The established timelines of the franchise, far from being impervious to change, frequently get altered by later writers within the stories themselves in a kind of narrative call-and-response. The inherently disruptive nature of time travel in **Doctor Who** subverts rigid notions of canon and authority.

Even when multiple timelines are not mentioned in a specific **Who** story, they can be assumed as a possibility, a steady part of the franchise's background hum. Fans in their basements and creators on the payroll (and those who are both) all have the power to create new realities for themselves and to say 'time can be rewritten'.

This makes the franchise into what the field of fandom studies calls an 'archontic' story[104] – an archive in which no text is ever complete. Philosopher Jacques Derrida has summarised how by 'incorporating the knowledge deployed in reference to it, the archive augments itself, engrosses itself' but 'in the same stroke it loses the absolute and metatextual textual authority it might claim to have'[105].

The **Target Library** novelisations present new interpretations of TV episodes; audio plays, stage shows, comics, books and candy merchandise show us diverging histories, alternative futures and

---

[103] Marchon, Alex, personal correspondence.
[104] Basu, 'When Worlds Continue', p171, building on theories by literary scholar Abigail Derecho (now publishing as Abigail DeKosnik) and philosopher Jacques Derrida.
[105] Derrida, Jacques, *Archive Fever: A Freudian Impression*, p68.

even brand new Doctors. And the TV series constantly gathers up such transformative ideas and re-iterates them – meaning there is not necessarily any conflict when the Doctor experiences Paul Cornell's 1995 novel *Human Nature* in his seventh incarnation, and the re-imagined 2007 TV story of the same name many bodies later. The unfolding story's possibilities become literally endless.

The focus on time travel allows all media within the franchise to co-exist as separate timelines. Several versions can be told of a single story, and contradictory takes can drift peacefully side by side or mutually influence each other. This system has even become a necessity rather than just creative fancy: no writer would ever be able to consume, remember and implement every plot element in all these decades' worth of multimedial lore. The Doctor himself said it best, appropriately enough in one of the novels:

> 'What if the "real" timeline is like a musical score, with infinite ornamentations possible? There can't be a perfectly correct performance of the score, because a score is a guide, not a definition. It opens possibilities rather than closing them off. Why shouldn't time be like music?'[106]

Every addition to the saga has the potential to shift the ways in which the series' past and future interact, rather than actually invalidating anything. Like the TARDIS travellers, the fans-turned-writers have the power to saunter into known history and change it, or to add new meaning to old stories, or to simply jump a time track within the lore and create parallel histories wherever they please.

---

[106] Rose, Lloyd, *Camera Obscura*, p172.

The result is that **Doctor Who**'s time travel itself disrupts the culturally constructed notion that only those works approved by an elite should be allowed into some inflexible form of canon: the notion that someone like the Abzorbaloff could assert absolute dominance over the creativity of fans like LINDA. Even as the Abzorbaloff tries to overrule their fannish interpretations and ornamentations, cutting short their performance of ELO's score in apt symbolism when he comes barging into their lives, they always retain the power eventually to defy him.

Myth Makers and Time Ravagers

Fan communities can branch out from gift economies into monetised exchanges of fan output. **Doctor Who** has a decades-long tradition of works that lack the necessary licences, but which are still commercialised and marketed to **Who**'s fandom. The hero in such works may be called 'the Professor' or 'the Stranger' to swerve around lawyers. Often, the Doctor is peripheral or absent as unexpected characters (not unlike Elton and his friends) step into the foreground instead. But the mother franchise is not by definition an enemy to this exchange model: quite frequently, the BBC or other licence holders have looked the other way to let commercial fan works roam free even as they 'broke every copyright rule in the book'[107].

Instead of having profit for the franchise's owners as a major goal, this type of fan production is carried out directly for use and affective consumption by the fandom, with any proceeds providing means to charities and further community projects. Their contents can flow

---

[107] Mammone, Rob, 'Gary Russell talks about the **Audio Visuals**'.

into explicit canonicity as licensed adventures subsequently build on them – whether through appropriation, in direct cooperation with their originators, or by said originators themselves.

Certain thresholds do exist. For example, a fan work based on **Doctor Who** that's published for free directly by its creator will typically not be considered part of the lore But such a work can still gain 'validity' in the eyes of fans when its author also creates licensed material, or when its contents are subsequently referenced or re-used in monetised works. Perhaps the most striking recent example is the Series 8 title sequence, which started life as a YouTube fanvid, with vidder Billy Hanshaw being signed by the BBC at Steven Moffat's enthusiastic behest[108].

But while financial transactions – the dynamic between labour and capital, rather than only between labour and social affection – seem to be the most accepted determinator of what's part of the franchise, even that barrier isn't clear-cut. This means that literally every fan work, even those created in dingy garages by LINDA-like geeks, has the **potential** to attach itself to the overall mythology. A lack of recognition by the franchise does not mean that the fans are, if you'll forgive the terrible pun, disenfranchised. The less official works can disrupt the social construct of canonicity by refusing to accept any timeline or canon as the standard and by questioning the supposed necessity that they define themselves in contrast with it. Utopian as it may seem, **Who** fandom can choose a model of thinking in which every creator and every work is simply part of the whole.

---

[108] Johnston, Connor, 'Interview: Billy Hanshaw On Series 8's Title Sequence'.

Some authors who move in these less official spheres openly question the way TV adventures (or other licensed tales) influence the public perception of **Doctor Who**, and write their own stories as acts of rebellion against specific plotlines, becoming the perpendicular warp to the BBC's weft. Others choose to happily bask in the existing stories. This process allows fans to either celebrate and join in the commercial mainstream of the series or, if they prefer, to simply walk away from the assumed authority of those ascended and 'professionalised' creators who aim to take control of the fandom and who, to quote Jenkins, 'sold fan texts back to the community they originated from as commodities'[109]. In Marxist terms, the power to be part of a knowledge community also brings with it the power to resist the commodity capitalism that values labour for exchange value above all else.

The very act of creating **Who** fan works, like LINDA symbolically do, is therefore revolutionary towards everything that came before it – and, in dialogue with its antecedents, can add new meaning to any part of the show's history. Even from a gatekeeping perspective where only certain stories are accepted as the canon, the franchise still inspires fannish fiction and non-fiction which, in return, can be built on by stories that do 'count' in someone's eyes[110]. And so, while

---

[109] Jenkins, *Textual Poachers*, p32.

[110] Examples include, but are in no way limited to: John Tulloch and Manuel Alvarado's *Doctor Who: The Unfolding Text* being jokingly quoted in *Dragonfire* (1987); 'The Night of the Doctor' (2013) naming several Big Finish companions; Kate Stewart first appearing in the Reeltime Pictures direct-to-video release *Downtime* (1995) and decades later becoming head of UNIT in the TV series; the Doctor

LINDA are excluded from the TARDIS world, as allegorical **Doctor Who** fan-creators they are **simultaneously** already an integral part of it, on their own terms.

This also casts a different light on the idea of Davies' 2005 series revival as a form of redistribution. After all, the mythos still existed in many different formats during the 'Wilderness Years' and would have continued to be told with or without the BBC's permission. Is it still redistribution if something already belongs to the masses?

Of course, TV licensing does grant stories one thing which unlicensed works typically don't have: the potential to reach a global audience willing to invest both emotionally and financially on a massive scale. By reviving the TV iteration of **Who**, Davies provided an enormous increase in output and reach for the whole franchise. But due to the nature of time in **Doctor Who**, his new stories amplified those created elsewhere and gave them a new context, rather than invalidating them or cutting the fan-creators off from the production of the overall story. Fans may baulk at those who take over the TV narrative, but we also know deep down that no super-fan, showrunner or Abzorbaloff can ever truly cornerstone the resources of the entire fandom – or impose any rigid demarcation on what's valid. The power to shape the story lies with **all** of **Who**'s fan culture.

David Tennant made himself into the poster boy for fans becoming part of what they love, stating in a 2003 interview:

> 'Oh, it's a real anorak admission. I've been an obsessive **Doctor Who** fan since I was a child and it persists to this very

---

alluding to the events of DWM's 'The World Shapers' (1987) in *The Doctor Falls* (2017).

day. The BBC run a **Doctor Who** website and I go on almost every day to check the latest news. **Doctor Who** is the finest piece of television that has ever been made anywhere. They're putting together a new TV series next year and [...] I've been onto my agent to see if I can get a part, but she's not keen. She says I'll never work again if I do it. I'm proud to say, though, that I have already performed in a couple of audiobook episodes. That was heaven.'[111]

From a little boy who dressed up as the Doctor[112] and carried a **Who** doll around, Tennant went on to write school essays about this show that made him want to act professionally[113], bothered fifth Doctor actor Peter Davison in a pub in 1993[114], started enthusiastically claiming his first **Who** parts in Big Finish spinoffs and tie-ins and BBC webcast material[115], and took on the part of the Doctor himself in 2005. Perhaps, with just a little bit of luck and better judgment, poor Elton would have been just as welcome as Tennant in everything he chased – instead of watching this Doctor's adventures from the wings.

---

[111] '20 Questions With... David Tennant'.
[112] Tennant: 'Very odd, when you grown up with something, when you've been a real, proper fan of something. With posters on your wall and my granny knitted me a long scarf and a cricket jumper... Extraordinary that all these years later that it should come sort of full circle...' Bone, Christian, 'David Tennant Reveals How He Was Offered The Role Of Doctor Who'.
[113] Wood, Jennifer M, '15 Surprising Facts About David Tennant'.
[114] As told by Davison at his c2e2 2013 panel.
[115] In the alternative timeline stories *Sympathy for the Devil* and *Exile* (both 2003), the **UNIT** series (2004-05), and the webcast *Scream of the Shalka* (2003).

Fans involved in transformative groups – such as the **Audio Visuals** crew, BBV Productions, Reeltime Pictures, Magic Bullet Productions, The Doctor Who Information Network, and Big Finish Productions – gradually secured various commissions and licences over the years to produce sanctioned **Who** audio plays, books, comics, analyses, artworks and films. Their initial partially-licensed or purely fannish works, created in their LINDA-like hubs, formed an integral part of that process. Their creations frequently ended up referenced or re-imagined later on in more official output – either by themselves or by others who in turn became inspired by these stories.

Taking all these possible roads within and without copyright, Davies and his fellow fans created their own transformative content. They built their skills in the media landscape, found their own niches as **Doctor Who** world-builders, and finally succeeded in bringing the TV series back on air. Fandom seized the means of TV production.

The two aspects of the TV creators' history as ascended fans are showcased in *Love & Monsters*, in the episode's geeky community on the one hand and in the hyper-consuming boss on the other. Looking at the Abzorbaloff's defeat, we can recognise the falsehood of the notion that one super-fan could possibly control the entire franchise – whether by becoming showrunner or just by ruthlessly hoarding knowledge. And looking back to LINDA, we can choose to see not just a group of outcasts cut off from the Doctor's life, but also a mirror of all those fans who once banded together over their shared passion and who now sit at the heart of the TV series.

Down Where We Used to Go

So in the end, did these ascended fans change the class nature of production? Or would it be more accurate to say that only their own class position changed? And have they commodified the series for the new establishment – as LINDA end up commodifying their fascination with the Doctor for the Abzorbaloff's gain – or has **Doctor Who** fandom broken free of such dynamics? These questions don't seem to have black-and-white answers.

All the way back in Weimar Republic Germany, Bertolt Brecht had some strong opinions on the topic of audience involvement. In his theories of applicability and media interaction, he claimed that fans should continuously rewrite existing stories across generations to suit their own circumstances, and to become the new creators of the media that they consume.

Davies echoes this sentiment: 'The best thing that a new team can do,' he writes on the topic of stepping down as showrunner, 'is move in, trample over the way that we did things, and find new ways for themselves.'[116] Decades before him, script editor Terrance Dicks expressed much the same thing, stating how:

> '[...] now that John Nathan-Turner and his script editor Eric Saward have taken over, they will do it differently, and it is quite right that they should. They should not do it the way I would do it, that is the whole point. And I think that is really the answer to what has kept **Doctor Who** alive – it's this continuous input.'[117]

Brecht meant for all art – including his own writing – to keep on being altered and defamiliarised by each generation of creators. This way, art would become an archontic dialogue, in which the voices of the

---

[116] Davies and Cook, *The Writer's Tale*, p127.
[117] Tulloch, John and Manuel Alvarado, *The Unfolding Text*, p3.

people could be constantly amplified to change all the old narratives. Brecht treated ideas such as copyright and narrative ownership like capitalist social constructs, certainly useful to reach audiences with, but which should be questioned and disrupted wherever possible. The playwright dreamed of a world in which every audience member could influence every single story and thereby change the media landscape around them[118].

I think no other fandom in the world has come close to that dream like **Doctor Who**'s has. As Balaka Basu says with grace, 'the barriers between these once carefully delineated hierarchies – fan and producer, producer and production, and fan and production – have become progressively more permeable' and the fact that today's **Doctor Who** TV creators identify as fans of the show, 'when coupled with the program's fannish theme of passionate engagement with media and fictions, creates an Ourobouros-like metatextual narrative that models and reflects the disappearing boundaries between creator, text, and audience'[119].

Basu points out that this fan-creation process is even seen in the characters: the 21st century Doctor and the companions, particularly Martha and Donna, are shown as self-professed fans of creators such as Charles Dickens, William Shakespeare and Agatha Christie, and are able to paradoxically shape these heroes' stories by inspiring them. 'It's axiomatic that the viewer gazes at the text', Basu says, but 'equally true, these days, is the fact that the text gazes back.' The

---

[118] An English overview of this can be found in *Brecht in Practice* as well as in Brecht's own writings collected in Willett, Jon, ed/trans, *Brecht on Theatre*.
[119] Basu, 'When Worlds Continue', p165.

power of fans goes beyond creating transformative works or pointing out flaws, and extends to transforming the core story itself[120].

Portrait by the Artist as a Young Man

Enter William Grantham, a nine-year-old artist and fan, who won a **Blue Peter** contest to design his own **Doctor Who** monster.

The two shows have a long history of mutual admiration and in 2005, **Blue Peter** editor Richard Marson offered young viewers the opportunity to design a monster for the Doctor to fight. Grantham's winning design was picked from 43,920 entries and announced on TV by Tennant[121].

It wasn't the first time a child had designed a monster for the Doctor. Among Grantham's predecessors had been more than 250,000 children who, in 1967, designed their own creatures for the BBC 'Make a Monster for Dr Who' competition. Three winners were selected to have their drawings made real by the **Doctor Who** props department. On **Blue Peter**, Karen Dagg contributed her Steel Octopus with 'explosive arms', Paul Worrall was proud of his reptilian Hypnotron that could 'transfix Daleks' and Stephen Thompson gave the world Aqwa Man, a sonic robot[122]. Second Doctor actor Patrick Troughton helped pick the winners and spoke encouragingly about the children to the press.

Grantham followed in the footsteps of these children when his pencil art was brought to life by Peter Kay. The behind-the-scenes BBC show **Doctor Who Confidential** was on the *Love & Monsters* set to film

---

[120] Basu, 'When Worlds Continue', pp171-2.
[121] **Blue Peter**, 17 August 2005.
[122] **Blue Peter**, 14 December 1967.

Grantham's wide-eyed joy as his drawing became reality. His encounter with Kay, narrated for **Confidential** by writer Mark Gatiss, was the ultimate fannish moment – a fan-run TV show about a TV show revived by fans, showing a fan meeting a fellow fan dressed up as his own fan creation symbolising a fan, who was set to fight the Doctor played by a fan, surrounded by fan characters, with the whole thing narrated by a fan.

The Savage

There's something else that needs to be discussed, and it's uncomfortable. But here we go. The black-mohawked, loincloth-clad Azorbaloff isn't just light-years away from the refined bourgeois front of 'Mr Kennedy' – he can also be seen as a walking racist stereotype. These design elements mark him out as a barbaric beast and (since they're taken from images of tribal peoples) conflate native dress, connotations of cannibalism and monstrous savagery.

We can't blame William Grantham here, of course. Most obviously because he was just a kid, but also because of how the monster's look was embellished by the costume design team. The tufts of hair in Jenkins' original drawing are only just barely a 'mohawk' hairstyle. The loincloth was meant to be a 'sumo' outfit in his eyes, not a tribal one[123]. (Which also invites race-related scrutiny, just of a different type.) But the way the production team chose to emphasise and exaggerate these aspects is unfortunate. While we don't know

---

[123] *The New World of Who*. Writer Alan Stevens (in personal correspondence) has also noted strong similarities in design between the Abzorbaloff and Grunthos the Flatulent from *Episode 2* of **The Hitchhiker's Guide to the Galaxy** (1981), which may indeed have been a direct inspiration.

whether this was intentional or a total accident, it perpetuates prejudice either way.

The racist imagery is worsened by the villain being blond when he presents as cultured, and only showing his black mohawk when revealed as a slobbering menace. The Russian-sounding name Abzorbaloff further codes him as foreign and therefore othered by association with a non-Western identity, and contrasts with the American-coded name Kennedy. His veil of fake Western identity hides a secret foreign core.

The classic horror story trope of the alien or monster as a symbolic immigrant, as an ethnic caricature from a distant land who imitates, infects, ingests, taints and/or replaces the genteel English populace, is in full force here. Whether it was vampires crossing into Britain to exchange foreign bodily fluids with helpless ingénues, or werewolves transforming regular people into hairy savages with a single bite, Western media have long since found creative ways to make monsters stand in for the 'threat' of foreigners 'infecting' whiteness.

It's also telling that when we finally see the Abzorbaloff attack, he absorbs Ursula via her **arm** – as Kate Orman examines in her **Black Archive** on *Pyramids of Mars* (1975), baddies who symbolise foreigners in British monster literature latch on to arms more often than to any other body part[124]. The wealthy public persona in contrast with the ravenous true form of the monster draws on the same traditions, invoking classic vampire tropes found for example in Le Fanu's *Carmilla* and of course in Count Dracula himself. With LINDA as the ingénu(e)s to be devoured and transformed, the picture

---

[124] Orman, Kate, **The Black Archive** #12: *Pyramids of Mars*, pp32ff.

is complete.

There are two notable counterpoints to these foreigner-attacks-whiteness connotations. The first is the Abzorbaloff's Bolton accent, which codes him as British despite his foreign appearance. The second would be the fact that Bliss, a black woman, is the first of LINDA to be absorbed. However, the script specifies Bliss as blonde[125] – plus, countering the 'monster as infectious foreigner' trope with the old 'black character dies first' horror chestnut doesn't help.

It's hardly the first time **Doctor Who** has used ethnic imagery to portray someone as savage and/or villainous. The violent and dim-witted Ogron servant race first appearing in *Day of the Daleks* (1972), with their dark brown skin and their big pink lips, big noses and heavy brow ridges are the most awkward example. Other instances include the titular villain of *The Celestial Toymaker* (1966) displaying Chinese culture as some Fu Manchu style, White Peacock mystic menace; Louise Jameson wearing brown contacts to play 'savage' tribal companion Leela[126]; and more recently the entire planet of Shan Shen reviving the orientalist 'evil Asian fortune tellers' cliché – cunning Dragon Lady and all – in *Turn Left* (2008). As fans, we have the power to acknowledge these things, to be critical of them when they occur, and to create more compassion in our fandom[127].

---

[125] *The Complete History* #53, p54.
[126] See also Thomas Rodebaugh's **Black Archive** on *The Face of Evil* (1977) for detailed discussion of Leela's skin tone.
[127] As a white author living in a predominantly white society, I acknowledge that others know much more about racism than I do. The essays collected by Lindy Orthia in *Doctor Who and Race* offer further information.

The Interplay of Attraction and Repulsion

The Abzorbaloff's predecessors in **Doctor Who** also include the Foamasi from *The Leisure Hive* (1980) and, as Rose points out, Davies' Raxacoricofallapatorians first seen in *Aliens of London*. All three alien types are large, green, three-fingered bipeds who combine themselves with humans. All three create the illusion of being wealthy and powerful through their disguises: the Foamasi by presenting as respectable businesspeople, the Slitheen family of Raxacoricofallapatorians by wearing government officials as skin suits, and the Abzorbaloff in his upper-class Kennedy persona. The connection between the Abzorbaloff and the Raxacoricofallapatorians, whose home planets are twinned, is especially interesting because of another factor they have in common: grossout comedy.

At its core, grossout comedy is where humour and horror intersect. We're simultaneously drawn in by the jokes and repulsed by the sensory aspects of them, such as disgusting visuals, unpleasant bodily functions or (the mention of) nasty smells. This narrative game of push and pull can be used to great effect. The Slitheen and the Abzorbaloff are silly and disgusting at the same time – attractive as something to laugh at, and repulsive as something we'd never want to be anywhere near. The fear of them crawling into our skins or, conversely, absorbing us into their own bodies (two sides of the same coin in horror terms) becomes more immediate, more tangible, as we find ourselves also lured in by how funny they are.

Of course, the corollary is that when viewers **don't** find these monsters funny... the horror can fall flat on its face as well. Which leads into another unpleasant aspect of the episode that needs to be mentioned.

One thing in particular sets the Slitheen and the Abzorbaloff apart: the kind of nudity that we see. The neotenous Raxacoricofallapatorians are naked the way monsters are naked. But the Abzorbaloff, with his loincloth, his exaggerated pecs and his disturbingly man-like face, is (practically) naked the way an **adult human** is naked. Combined with his incessant lip-licking, his references to how his victims will 'taste' and the extremely awkward connotations of him asking his pupils to stay behind after class, what the story ends up with is a baddie who comes across as a sexual predator. The fact that he literally forces Bliss' face onto his bum doesn't help.

This whole vibe can make it harder for viewers to laugh at his antics, and gives off a sense of discomfort far beyond that of just seeing an alien beast. What we may see instead is realistic danger. If the Abzorbaloff had been less humanoid, less teacher-like and less preoccupied with his own tongue maybe both his comedy and his horror would have found a broader audience.

The Self-Aware Monster

The Slitheen and the Abzorbaloff additionally represent something more metafictional: the idea of **Doctor Who** monsters being utterly rubbish. To what extent that prejudice is justified is a little beyond the scope of this book, but over the years, budget constraints and unfortunate designs have often caused the monsters to look ridiculous. Davies found ways to implement these parts of the series' reputation in the show as self-aware elements, and to make them work for his 21st century audience. They can be a wink and nod to long-time fans as if saying, look, we all know this is a silly show and we're going to **celebrate** that silliness.

The show's monsters weren't the only thing that got a bad reputation in the 20th century – the fans suffered equally, being widely seen as obnoxious and obsessed anoraks. Their enthusiasm for the show was perceived to, in turn, make the writing cater to the fandom in ways that confused and excluded more casual viewers. To quote McNaughton, the show 'had become characterised as a programme that only fans could enjoy'[128]. Because of this, the Slitheen and the Abzorbaloff as self-aware exaggerations of the 'ridiculous **Doctor Who** monster' prejudice are not too different from *Love & Monsters*' self-aware exaggerations of the 'rubbish **Doctor Who** fan'.

Such camp sensibilities contribute to *Love & Monsters* being seen as a 'breather' episode – as an inconsequential bit of fluff, cushioning the series' actual plot. But that approach is too reductive. 'Another way of looking at it', as Sandifer states, 'is that the Abzorbaloff is perfectly sized for Elton's tiny little world.'[129]

Zeff approached the script not as a comedy but as a dark fairy tale, comparing it to the 1990 romantic film *Edward Scissorhands*[130]. Davies intended for the story to be relatable and instructed the cast to 'keep it real'[131]. And although Kay ad-libbed some jokes (like Kennedy's inability to pronounce 'eczema'[132]), he aimed to play his character as menacing rather than just funny, and to keep the piece

---

[128] McNaughton, 'Regeneration of a Brand', p 194.
[129] Sandifer, 'Their Little Groups'.
[130] *The Complete History* #53, p53.
[131] *The Complete History* #53, p55.
[132] *Love & Monsters* DVD commentary.

genuine[133]. Any story can be humorous and scary at once – in fact, to quote Sandifer again, it's 'the abandonment of the silliness' which *Love & Monsters* sets up in act 1 that makes the horror in the second half work all the better[134].

---

[133] *The Complete History* #53, p53.
[134] Sandifer, 'Their Little Groups'.

CHAPTER 5: 'WE'VE GOT THE PLACE TO OURSELVES'

A Day in the Limelight for Jackie

The process of mixing comedy and horror maps onto the art of mixing comedy and tragedy as well. A story can attract its viewers with easy laughter and, as soon as they're hooked, proceed to break their hearts. Davies, an experienced soap opera writer and storyliner, understands how interlinked the two can be:

> 'I hate saying Comedy and Drama, because it automatically assumes that Drama = Tragedy. Big, big mistake. Drama encompasses the whole range. But I believe passionately that Comedy and Tragedy exist alongside each other. No way are they diametric opposites; they're right next to each other, and they overlap in a thousand different ways.'[135]

Family drama is the perfect backdrop for these scenes. In leading up to the interplay of comedy and grief seen in *Love & Monsters*, Davies seeded aspects of Jackie Tyler throughout the first two series that would make such a development believable:

> 'I have to write like that. Funny, sad, all at once. That's how life is. You can have a pratfall at a funeral. You can laugh so much that you choke to death. [...] Jackie Tyler makes us laugh, but I knew that I'd uncover something sad at the heart of her. Her sadness over her absent daughter is there as early as *Aliens of London*, but you don't really get to see it properly until *Love & Monsters*. Idiots will say, "Ah, that character is

---

[135] Davies and Cook, *The Writer's Tale*, p129.

developing now" – what, like you were going to play it all in the first 30 seconds?! – but that capacity was always there. It had to be. Even in *Rose*, when Jackie is ostensibly 'funny', telling her daughter to get a job in the butcher's, Jackie is one of the things that's holding Rose back – and that's quite dark, at its heart. "Funny" is hiding a lot of other stuff.'[136]

Davies' fascination with mums gives them a lot of screentime in his era. This is one of the major things setting his vision on the show apart from its 20th-century storytelling. Most TARDIS travellers in the old days were lucky if their relatives were even mentioned; if they did show up, as did Nyssa's father Tremas or Tegan's aunt Vanessa, they were unlikely to survive[137]. While *The Curse of Fenric* (1989) gave a little more depth to Ace's mother and grandmother, they didn't appear on TV again afterwards.

Being a mum in Davies' stories is treated as a separate social role from that of the other characters. His portrayal of mothers is conflicted: on the one hand, he gets them involved in the stories more than most action-oriented TV shows dare to, but on the other hand he has trouble fitting them into active roles. Writing *Journey's End* (2008), he nearly left Jackie out of the action scenes because he couldn't imagine her defending the planet with a baby at home. When he eventually did include her, describing her thoughts as 'I'm not staying behind! Where's my daughter!?', his decision came with a great big dollop of misogyny: 'Like a nag.'[138]

Still, the way Davies writes Jackie shows a deep love for the character.

---

[136] Davies and Cook, *The Writer's Tale*, p129.
[137] *The Keeper of Traken* and *Logopolis* (both 1981).
[138] Davies and Cook, *The Writer's Tale*, p313.

The idea of weaving a companion's mother into the plot of his **Doctor Who** revival came from his frustration watching **Buffy** and seeing the titular character's mother, Joyce, continuously left out. He explains:

> 'In the architecture of it, I would have had Buffy's mum much more involved. And I was always watching it thinking, well come on, Joyce, let's get involved in the story. And so here you get my own show, and so the time's ripe. Jackie, in you come [...] This is gonna be right at the heart of it.'[139]

The mothers in his episodes provide an anchoring role, a home for the companions to return to. But they also root the adventures in true-to-life experiences and make the world of the series more recognisable, precisely by being the people who – like us – stay back in reality. Jackie even calls herself one of 'those who get left behind'. This makes Jackie's position similar to that of Elton – the everyday person on the sidelines, largely missing out on the action.

Elton essentially tries to take on another version of Jackie's role. He wants to become a part of the Doctor's and Rose's lives just like Jackie is, someone that they would want to fly to and talk to and feel comfortable with. What he fails to realise is that if you place someone on a pedestal, you make that person look down on you. He offers nothing that the TARDIS travellers would actually want to be near. Jackie succeeds where Elton fails in having access to the Doctor and Rose, even though she's left out of their space adventures – not through any fannish obsession, but simply by being Rose's mum.

Interestingly, *Love & Monsters* wasn't always a vehicle for Jackie. It was only when the character concept of Elton changed from female

---

[139] **Toby Hadoke's Who's Round** #54.

to male that Davies decided to include her. He felt that the episode's mundane setting was a good place to explore her life, and that her femininity would contrast well with Elton as a man. Given that she would leave **Doctor Who** at the end of the season, it was the perfect moment to give her a significant role[140].

Keeping Mum

Sandifer perfectly describes Jackie's function in the series:

> 'Jackie has always been a character the audience is meant to have complex opinions on, because she's consciously designed both as an impediment to **Doctor Who** getting up to full speed and as a character who fundamentally rejects a swath of the values of **Doctor Who**. She doesn't want a world of aliens and monsters and epic bombast; she wants the peace and quiet of the ordinary. As such, **Doctor Who** is fundamentally hostile to her. There's no way to get over the central conflict she introduces to the series, which is that she wants Rose to stay home and neither Rose nor, more importantly, the viewing public agrees.'[141]

Jackie is the face of normalcy in **Who** – the everywoman who makes the Doctor's world believable in *Rose*, appearing in entire scenes before the Doctor himself even shows up. Rather than being a one-note figure, though, she's a complex mix of traits making up a layered character. She's not the kind of woman who's put into narrative stasis as soon as she's off-screen. We have no trouble imagining Jackie living her everyday life while Rose is off exploring space. This

---

[140] Sullivan, Shannon Patrick, 'Love & Monsters'.
[141] Sandifer, 'Their Little Groups'.

is why Jackie's presence in *Love & Monsters* is a continuation of what's already been established. She's the logical bridge between Elton's world and that of the TARDIS – one foot firmly planted in normal life, and one foot in **Doctor Who**.

Camille Coduri chose to play Jackie as 'vulnerable' and 'girly' for this story. While previous episodes such as *Aliens of London* and *Father's Day* (2005) already showed us her raw emotions, here for the first time we see her without Rose by her side. As Coduri explains: 'You're never the same when your children aren't there. You're not the same mother. You become a complete individual.'[142] *Love & Monsters* humanises her in ways that are usually closed off to recurring satellite characters. Here, she can be motherly without impeding Rose's space adventures, and sexual without being rebuffed by the Doctor like she was in her first appearance. Her advances in Elton's direction are genuine and sweet rather than a throwaway joke. Davies also mentions deliberately not having her play the sad widow card, instead presenting her sexual desire as something joyful[143].

There are interesting implications to a sudden focus on Jackie (twice-removed from the Doctor in terms of character constellations), when the audience expects to see the Doctor and Rose featured front and centre. She's a bridge between mundanity and **Doctor Who**, not just for Elton but also for the viewers. Here, her connection to the Doctor and Rose becomes a teasing carrot waved in front of our noses – one step closer back into the regular narrative that we watch the series for, but still never quite getting there. Sandifer points out that, much

---

[142] *Love & Monsters* DVD commentary.
[143] *Love & Monsters* DVD commentary, The Complete Second Series edition.

like Elton being a replacement hero while Piper and Tennant are off making the filming schedule work, Jackie strikes a balance between being an intrusion in the series' flow and a facilitator thereof[144].

We need Jackie to be believable in order for this setup to work. Davies achieves this by fleshing her out and developing her surroundings. Throughout the story, we get to know her taste in music, see her friends from around the estate, hear how others view her and her daughter, and become part of her world for a little while. The explicit mention of Jackie's home address anchors her even more strongly in reality. *Love & Monsters* was the first time in **Who**'s TV history that a character like her was given such a strong, heartfelt platform to just live her everyday life.

Because we're asked to feel for her – maybe even to make ourselves at home with her – Elton's betrayal of her hits all the harder. The breach of trust in itself is just as powerful as Jackie's realisation that this was never about her to begin with. She finds herself made into a commodity in a thoroughly Brechtian way, a victim of Elton's unnecessary choice to corrupt his social relations for the Abzorbaloff's goals.

Elton makes himself (or more specifically his body) into a commodity as well, in his willingness to trade sex with Jackie for knowledge-based capital. By nearly prostituting himself in order to gain resources for his boss, he strongly evokes Brecht's narrative portrayals of whores, who in turn signify the Marxist notion of workers in capitalist society who 'daily and hourly must sell

---

[144] Sandifer, 'Their Little Groups'.

themselves'[145].

All that's left of Jackie in the episode's final minutes is her role as an unseen plot motivator: the Doctor only interacts with the climax so that Rose can shout at Elton for upsetting her mum. When Jackie says goodbye to Elton, she's once again relegated to being a side character. Her purpose in his eyes was to provide a link to the Doctor and Rose and to guide him into **Doctor Who** proper. Jackie's earlier phone call with Rose (happening mostly offscreen, to add another layer of alienation) reminds us of all the loneliness that's part of Jackie's world. So much of her life is spent longing for people – for her husband Pete, who died; for Rose, who's off in space; and for this fit young man who's willing to help around the house but who just isn't the guy he claimed to be.

This thread of unfulfilled longing runs through the entire episode. Much as Elton yearns for a fantasy image of the Doctor that he's built up in his mind since childhood, Jackie is hungry to get close to a fantasy image of Elton which is little more than a front for his actual goals. Elton claims that it's not 'like that' and that he was genuine in his friendship with her, which may well be true, but in the end his secrecy casts him out from her life again just like he's already been cast out from the rest of **Doctor Who**. 'Because,' as Jackie tells us, 'it's hard. And that's what you become. Hard.'

The Other Mother

With all that focus on Jackie, we could almost forget Elton's reason

---

[145] Engels, Friedrich and Karl Marx, *Manifest der Kommunistischen Partei* ['Manifesto of the Communist Party'], p60.

for hunting the Doctor: he was there when Elton's own mum died.

And here, we suddenly see another factor that could have made Elton feel so comfortable stalking Jackie. His entire quest to find the Doctor and Rose was already deep down a quest for a mother, and in Jackie he finds someone much closer to his actual goal than the 10th Doctor could ever be. When our geeky new lead enters Jackie's world, away from the abandoned streets and the battered basement and into the hustle and bustle of her life, we could imagine him walking into the welcoming arms of motherhood itself.

What Elton searches for isn't so much the Doctor as a person, but the Doctor as a way to receive closure for his mother's death. (And perhaps symbolically, as a fan, seeking narrative closure for a plot thread left unresolved or for a missing episode still lost.) It's revealed in the final few minutes that *Love & Monsters* was a murder mystery all along. Elton has made his new group of friends into the London Investigation 'N' Detective Agency because he **needs** to be a detective – because he needs to solve this crime.

Surrounding himself with classic British detective story elements such as ordinary London streets, calm conversations about the suspect and cosy domestic scenes, he follows the genre's traditions by narrating the unfolding mystery to his unseen, unresponsive audience. This also adds more meaning to how normal his little world's backdrop is. As Lamerichs describes, murder mystery as a plot element 'changes an ordinary landscape into an active place of imagination, a story that slowly reveals itself'[146].

---

[146] Lamerichs, *Productive Fandom*, page 86, building on theories by cultural studies scholar Stijn Reijnders.

The flashbacks to his mother's life and passing, and the Doctor's explanation of how she was killed, are scenes with genuine emotion. We experience Elton's grief with soft light and gentle music, the Doctor's familiar narrating voice allowing us a glimpse back into **Doctor Who**'s regular story structure just for this one tender moment.

Elton's mother is something of a MacGuffin, however. She's not given a voice or a name, and her presence within the narrative seems to exist only to give Elton the emotions necessary to sustain the plot. Within *Love & Monsters*, and especially considering the loving focus on Jackie's life, this seems innocuous enough. After all, there's only so much space in the episode to explore each character. But in the larger context of fiction, there is still a disproportionate amount of stories which 'fridge' female characters (hurt, depower or kill them) for the purpose of exploring the grief of a male one[147]. Elton's mum fits into this pattern, and she's far from alone in **Doctor Who**.

Still, it's rare for motherhood and related emotions to be explored at all in sci-fi, let alone realistically. Davies was likely inspired here as well by the relationship between Buffy and her mum. Joyce's death in *The Body* (2001) was portrayed with a level of realism and mourning that stood in stark contrast to all of **Buffy**'s exciting murder scenes, its supernatural resurrections, and the narrative power which Buffy herself otherwise held over people's fates.

The grief that Elton feels for his mother comes across as genuine –

---

[147] A term coined by comics writer Gail Simone in 1999 after yet another female character, Alexandra DeWitt, was killed to elicit a response in a male one. Alexandra became the trope namer by being stuffed into a refrigerator: see the 'Women in Refrigerators' website.

and we're acutely aware that her unseen killer, an 'Elemental Shade' from the 'Howling Halls', might as well have been named 'car accident' or 'illness' or just 'loss'. Being voiceless and barely defined, she also becomes free to embody people in our own families who've died. Elton's quest for closure is recognisable precisely because the how and why of her death are immaterial – the sci-fi element being just thin wrapping paper for realistic grief. Moments like these, as Sandifer puts it, allow viewers 'to reclaim death from the realm of the epic' and to simply feel them for everything they are[148].

Lost Girls

And then there's the third mother in the story: Bridget.

'I started all of this because my daughter disappeared,' Bridget tells her new friends. 'It wasn't aliens that took her away. It was just drugs. I come down to London every week, and I just keep looking for her.'

Had Bridget been in any other **Doctor Who** episode, her daughter might have disappeared in glamorous combat with alien masterminds, or might even just have followed a traveller into a police box to see the universe. But Bridget's daughter doesn't get a space adventure. And Bridget doesn't get to have the experiences that Jackie had – the fantasy resolution of *Aliens of London*, in which a long lost daughter is magically delivered back on her doorstep, safe and sound.

The parallels between Bridget's daughter and Rose run slightly deeper still. One scene in *Rose* mentions Jimmy Stone, Rose's ex-boyfriend: 'It's all Jimmy Stone's fault. I only left school because of

---

[148] Sandifer, 'Their Little Groups'.

him. Look where he ended up.'

Davies elaborates that Rose chose a life of adventure with Jimmy for five months instead of taking her A-levels, and ended up abandoned by him and in financial debt before finally returning home to her mum[149]. It would seem that Rose never even needed aliens or time machines to walk straight into danger. Bridget's realistic loss is a glimpse into how Jackie herself could have suffered, had Rose loved drugs as recklessly as she loved Jimmy.

When Bridget seeks more than just reality, when she tries to insert herself into the **Doctor Who** narrative (so to speak) by seeking the Doctor and by eventually sharing her grief with Kennedy, the villain's response is tellingly dismissive. 'Bridget,' he tells her, 'don't make this personal. I don't like to be touched, literally or metaphorically, thank you very much. I haven't got the time. Bleeding hearts outside!'

And so, Bridget ends up sidelined in every way. Her daughter didn't become a companion; she doesn't get a spotlight like Jackie or a loving flashback like Elton's mum; her big damn TV kiss is just a peck on the cheek; and even the villain doesn't care. Both within the episode's plot and on a metafictional level, she's the ultimate bystander.

---

[149] Davies, Russell T, 'Meet Rose', p38ff. This backstory is woven into Davies' Target novelisation of *Rose* as well.

CHAPTER 6: 'FETCH A SPADE!'
The Gaps in Doctor-Lite Storytelling

Speaking of bystanders...

While Elton's daily life is a mystery, with the episode presenting him as a stripped-down, bare-bones character, what the Doctor and Rose get up to during *Love & Monsters* also stays a mystery – to us, and to Elton. We're subjected to a dashed plot line which defies our expectations of what we should know about the characters' actions. We barely see Elton's daily life outside of his own bedroom and LINDA; LINDA never see the Doctor and Rose aside from their brief encounters; and we never see the Doctor and Rose experience a regular **Doctor Who** plot.

Since Rose's appearance is so brief, the episode deconstructs her into her core characteristics. She cares about her mum, she listens to people when they're sad, and she travels with the Doctor. She's fierce and she's gentle; selfish and kind; huggable and strong. She's well-dressed and she can make the Doctor fly the TARDIS to wherever she wants to go. Any aspects of her character beyond those are taken as read. Viewers for whom *Love & Monsters* is their first ever Rose story would take away little about her from the narrative – her absence defines her more than her presence does.

Even Rose's anger, aimed at Elton by the episode's end, is sparked in off-screen conversation between her and Jackie. This means that her response to Elton is believable only to a certain extent. The writing sets up the emotional connection between her and Jackie, so it doesn't seem far-fetched that she'd go out of her way to scold Elton for upsetting her mum. But for her to ignore the Abzorbaloff and the situation surrounding the beast requires a thought process on her part (and the Doctor's, too) that we just don't witness. Are the TARDIS travellers deliberately ignoring the space monster, or don't they see the amount of horror in front of them? Are they playing a game to teach Elton a lesson? Is Elton's unreliable narration preventing us from seeing their true actions? Or are they both solidly on Elton's side, and trying to trick the Abzorbaloff from the moment they step out of the TARDIS? Is Rose in on it or is she shocked by the Doctor's words? How long have they been watching the chase, anyway?

In this scene, the Doctor and Rose become uncomfortable to us, because we can't understand how their response is being formed. We become forced to interpret them through their actions, rather than their inner lives. (Or to quote Brecht: 'What takes place inside of them must not be shown; the audience can conclude that for themselves.'[150]) Their cuddly monologuing session with Elton afterwards doesn't fully reel them back into our comfort zones. As we see them from Elton's viewpoint, they become strangers to us – harsh, volatile and alien.

Perhaps this harshness carries with it the Doctor's lingering fear of the Beast in *The Satan Pit*, having been confronted with his own mortality in the face of unimaginable power. Perhaps Rose's recent separation from the Doctor in that episode causes her to now stay by his side unquestioningly, afraid of losing him again. But as *Love & Monsters* declines to address its character dynamics outside of

---

[150] Brecht, Bertolt, 'Couragemodell 1949' ['Couragemodel 1949'] in Hecht, Werner et al, eds, *Bertolt Brecht: Schriften 5* ['Writings 5'], p228.

Elton's perspective, such speculation is entirely left up to the viewer.

The usual protagonists also play basically no part in the Abzorbaloff's defeat. While the TARDIS shows up in time to save Elton, the Doctor and Rose ultimately do little to help, and LINDA defeat the creature by themselves. All the Doctor provides is a distraction and one tiny hint – 'the others might have something to say' – making Ursula realise that they can pull the Abzorbaloff apart. There's absolutely no narrative reason for the Doctor to do things this way, pretending that he would let Elton die and giving a hint with such a slim chance of being correctly deciphered. But it doesn't matter, because if Ursula is clever enough to understand what the Doctor means, she could have also reached the same conclusion without his input. The destruction of the monster's body is a group effort that might have succeeded with or without the TARDIS there. The Doctor and Rose's most basic of roles in the series, that of the heroes, ends up cast aside.

Maybe this symbolises how our childhood heroes can't help us when we're all grown up – how the people we're fans of are unlikely to actually interfere in our own lives. Maybe it's a celebration of the power of fandom, or even a metaphor for the horror of a fan community literally falling apart. Maybe, conversely, it symbolises the artificial divide between fandom and canon in placing the Doctor above the conflict and thereby lampshading the supposed invulnerability of the Doctor as the embodiment of the franchise. Maybe the Doctor's attitude of merely inspiring the fans from a distance deliberately contrasts with the Abzorbaloff consuming every part of fandom that he touches[151]. Maybe Elton's making it all

---

[151] A theory put forth by Booy, *Love and Monsters*, p176ff.

up. With everything going on in this sequence, and our utter lack of access to the Doctor's thought process, we're free to pick any of these interpretations (and tons more besides).

It's worth pointing out that at the time of *Love & Monsters*, the Doctor under Davies had rarely taken the specific action that saved the day, with this role usually falling to other characters – but his inaction in other stories had been explained, whereas here it's incomprehensible.

In the next Doctor-lite story *Blink*, all these effects are much less extreme. Writer Steven Moffat was nervous to throw himself 'onto the grenade of the unpopular episode and do the low-budget Doctor-light one' and carefully avoided having his protagonist and structure be too much like *Love & Monsters*[152]. In contrast to Elton, his Sally Sparrow is immediately shown to have a social life outside of anything Doctor-related. The Doctor and Martha are said to have adventures ('four things and a lizard') that, unlike the generic Hoix, leave enough to the imagination to be thrilling. The narrative gaps that we're asked to fill in throughout *Blink* stimulate our creativity and interact with Sally's actions to create a complete story, whereas the Doctor's off-screen actions in *Love & Monsters* are mostly unrelated to LINDA's plot. On top of that, where Elton might be easy to identify with because his daily life stays a total blank space for us to imagine, Sally is easy to identify with simply because she could be our best mate.

Blink also gave us more constant access to the Doctor, by scattering him throughout the episode. Even when we only see him in recorded

---

[152] Arnopp, Jason, 'Steven Moffat On Writing'.

form, we feel closer to him than we can in *Love & Monsters* – because although we know that it's Sally he's addressing, not us, the DVD recording still gives us eye contact with our hero as well as continuous implicit requests from him to stay engaged with the plot. In comparison, the video footage and candid photographs of the Doctor and Rose in *Love & Monsters* are basically a cold shoulder. *Love & Monsters* may involve the audience in ways that *Blink* does not, but *Blink* never truly severs its viewers from the title character.

Despite *Blink*'s intense popularity, televised **Who** declined to do another double-banked episode without an established character as the protagonist again. Recurring companion Donna Noble took on the heroine role in the double-banked *Turn Left* (to have two units running, one with Tennant, one with Tate), foregoing the need to get the audience interested in a brand new lead.

Protagonist-Centred Morality

The Doctor is a good person. Usually. Alright, sure – at times our hero will lie, or steal, or commit murder, or pretend to regenerate and then laugh in Bill's face for no discernible reason[153]. But nobody's perfect. Right? We tend to forgive the Doctor for nearly everything, simply because the show presents him/her as the heroic protagonist. The title character stands in opposition to the forces of evil and must therefore be not evil. Whenever the Doctor truly ruins someone's life, it's often presented as an accident, or as a reason for our hero subsequently to suffer the consequences and make amends. The Doctor's mistakes are for the Do43 ctor to face and to feel and to fix, since even when straying into villainous territory, he/she is also still

---

[153] *The Lie of the Land* (2017).

the protagonist who must then react to those mistakes. Therefore, the Doctor isn't a proper antagonist in the show's usual structure – after all, that requires a new hero to step in and become the opposer, the sufferer and the fixer in response.

Some characters have opposed the Doctor in that sense over the years, if typically in brief bursts. An early example was seen in *The Edge of Destruction* (1964) in which companion Barbara Wright called the Doctor out on his behaviour. Another variation was seen between the secretive and manipulative seventh Doctor and his companion Ace, who was never afraid to confront him when he went too far. But the Doctor always got the final word in.

In *Aliens of London*, Jackie's realistic grief over her disappeared daughter finally transplanted the consequences of the Doctor's actions into our everyday circumstances proper. Jackie's loss of her child and the exploration of her feelings were realistic to a degree that felt intrusive in the sci-fi world of **Who**. Davies emphasised the impact on those on the sidelines in ways the 20th century series had rarely touched on. And while the Doctor had a very nice sci-fi explanation for taking Rose away from her mum for a year, to people like Jackie, and like us, no outer space excuse would truly matter – the grief would still be just as real. This story arc laid bare the fallout of the Doctor's life in a tangible setting, and was a prelude to themes that *Love & Monsters* would showcase a season later.

The structure of *Love & Monsters* allows this exploration to a degree that would otherwise be impossible. As a momentary protagonist, away from all the Doctor's reassuring babble, Elton guides us through the effects the Doctor has on those around him. In doing so, Elton automatically becomes a counterpoint, even an opponent, to the Doctor as he suffers the consequences of the Doctor's travels. Elton's perspective allows us to see the Doctor's actions from the sidelines, and to critically examine the trauma left in the Doctor's wake, without us being 'with' the Doctor again by the time the credits roll.

The Doctor is not just the absent hero, but is also among *Love & Monsters*' antagonists. Or, to put it another way, the Doctor and Elton serve as unintentional antagonists to each other while both still being protagonists to us. It's important to keep in mind that while Elton is **coded** as a fan, his relationship to the Doctor is not that of a fan to his idol – rather, it's that of a detective to his suspect, of a conspiracy theorist to his mastermind, of a cultist to his Nyarlathotep. At no point does he present the Doctor as flawless or even necessarily as good[154]. For Elton, the Doctor is a force of chaos – a mystery that he wants to draw out into the open. It's ironic, in a sense, that his ultimate goal in seeking the Doctor is to reclaim the comfort of his mother's memory, seeing as the Doctor's unwillingness to be pinned down to one place makes him the precise opposite of that calm, nostalgic and domestic life. Elton tries to tether himself to the untetherable traveller, and ends up emotionally adrift as a result.

When the Doctor is this inaccessible to the audience, does the mask of heroism start to crack a little? Are we more likely to acknowledge moments where he has failed? For example, maybe we feel that the

---

[154] Although the original script casts a different light on the story, with Elton stating: 'Funny thing is, I saw the Doctor, that night, with my mum, and even as a kid, I never thought it was his fault. I trusted him, even then.' *The Complete History* #53, p63.

Doctor should have stayed with young Elton longer after the Elemental Shade attack that killed his mother, instead of leaving the boy to cope with this trauma without closure. (Assuming that Elton even remembers these events correctly despite his age and the sudden shock of losing his mum, and tells it to us faithfully, that is.) The image of the Doctor standing silently in Elton's living room, alone and without the humanising presence of a companion, is haunting.

Maybe we also feel that the Doctor should have put more effort into protecting humans from nasties like the Abzorbaloff – after all, he's fully aware that people near him become beacons for nefarious space monsters. He even once told Mickey Smith to erase all information on him from the internet so that people wouldn't seek him out, because 'I'm dangerous. Don't want anybody following me.'[155] But even this was an example of the Doctor's negligence: he never made sure that the online information on him was actually deleted, which in turn enabled Ursula's website to keep existing, indirectly giving us the gift of LINDA.

Although questions like these are made possible by the setup, Elton is too much of a nice bloke to stay angry at the Doctor. 'It's not his fault', our ersatz protagonist tells us. Because of this, the discomfort of seeing Elton representing us as fans may not only lie in his methods to reach the Doctor, but also in his refusal of this power inherent to fandom. The 'challenge'[156] attitude of fannish activities

---

[155] *World War Three* (2005). The BBC website 'Who Is Doctor Who?' has Mickey stating that he refused to use the erasure disc: 'I can't bring myself to use it. You see, he's off, making another decision for us, all "I'm the big bad wolf and it's way past your bedtime." Well, I don't think so. Not this time.'
[156] Jenkins, *Textual Poachers*, p72.

towards the objects of fascination, as described by Henry Jenkins, is pretty much lacking in him. Fandom's 'refusal of authorial authority'[157] stays rather untapped as Elton never truly questions the Doctor (and only confronts the Abzorbaloff when it's far too late). And the horror of the fallout surrounding the Doctor never gets fully explored in this episode, as despite everything, Elton chooses to leave us on a positive note.

While later episodes do take things further – for example, when the Jones family become enslaved by the Master just for being related to companion Martha[158] – again we find ourselves emotionally and cinematographically by the Doctor's side once the episode ends. We're safely back in the TARDIS, expected to believe that all of the resulting trauma will just kind of sort itself out. Martha's family are assumed to recover from their year of torture (a single line in **Torchwood** states they're 'getting better'[159]) and are subsequently all but forgotten, save for a cameo by Francine in 2008's *The Stolen Earth / Journey's End*. Davies claims that 'Francine and Clive and Tish are changed forever' and 'life will never be the same again' for them[160], but if this in any way impacts the Doctor's choices afterwards, it doesn't show.

As Jon Arnold points out in his **Black Archive** on *The Eleventh Hour* (2010), the story of companion Amy Pond finally explores the things that *Love & Monsters* (among other stories) swerves around[161]. The

---

[157] Jenkins, *Textual Poachers*, p72.
[158] *Last of the Time Lords* (2007).
[159] **Torchwood**: *Reset* (2008).
[160] Cook, Benjamin, 'Leader Of The Gang', DWM #386, p18.
[161] Arnold, Jon, *The Eleventh Hour*, pp45ff.

fan-coded Amy and her partner Rory are both determined to call the Doctor out on his habit of running off, taking things in his stride, and pretty much just winging it.

Whereas Elton is content to get a hug from Rose and a brief monologue from the Doctor, little orphan Amy suffers a decade of explicitly mentioned psychological trauma when her Doctor leaves her behind, and continues to confront him about this throughout the series. And whereas *Love & Monsters* declines to address how the Doctor could have taken more steps to prevent people from being harmed, Rory scathingly tells the Doctor that he should have checked whether things were safe in *The Girl Who Waited* (2011), resulting in one of the rawest lines in **Doctor Who** history – 'That is not how I travel.'

The question is whether Elton would have had the narrative agency to say such things. After all, he barely gets to know the Doctor. We also lack the kind of emotional bond with him that recurring characters can form with audiences over time, so maybe we wouldn't even have listened if he'd been as blunt and confrontational as Amy and Rory. Maybe if Elton had said such things to the Doctor's face, we would have dismissed him for being a one-off, intrusive element in the show, with no right to call the Doctor out like that. Or maybe a one-off character would need to be a beautiful woman, or a dead one, or both, before the message would have enough impact – along the lines of Captain Adelaide Brooke in *The Waters of Mars* (2009). But even during Brooke's terrifying suicide as a direct result of the Doctor's actions, the writing still needs the Doctor himself to say those pivotal words: 'I've gone too far.' Without that verbal acknowledgment, any call-out statement takes on a completely different narrative purpose – for example, that of dramatic irony (we know things the Doctor doesn't know), of opposition to the audience (we hear things about the Doctor we don't want to hear) or of metatextual commentary (we see patterns in the show the Doctor never sees).

And maybe, if Elton truly had confronted the Doctor, he would only have been lecturing a fake image of the Time Lord that he'd built up in his own mind from scraps of memory and blurry footage – while the real Doctor would have stood there unchanged, like windmills standing before Don Quixote.

Or the Art of Sinking in Pavements

Whether or not the characters accept their circumstances, every little bit of new perspective can help to change a narrative. Just for these 45 minutes, Elton's viewpoint disables what Shklovsky called automised perception – and the story questions our unthinking acceptance of familiar narrative elements.

Let's take a moment to explore what exactly Shklovsky meant with 'ostrannenye' or estrangement. With this term, he described the way mundane storytelling can drag things we've become accustomed to back into focus. When we get used to something, whether in a story or in reality, we often stop questioning it. A regular occurrence can seem normal to us simply because we've never been invited to ask why it's happening. And any story element can seem logical just because it's part of the fiction. We're quick to accept the most implausible narrative twists because the characters themselves act as if it all makes sense in-universe[162]. Using narrative estrangement,

---

[162] Or to quote Shklovsky's unwieldy phrasing, 'the convention lying at the heart of every work of art' is that 'the situations in question,

however, we can see these elements from a new angle, as if we're looking at them for the first time.

Shklovsky linked this into the art of digressing from an expected plot. This kind of narrative time dilation can defamiliarise the topics that the characters discuss. He described how lengthening a story with filler content or postponing the main storyline (e.g. in a serialised work) can additionally make production much easier. The sense of unfulfillment when unexpected characters hog the spotlight can purposely be invoked to keep audiences wanting more, even when the main plot arcs are set aside completely.

Stating that 'the canonized [work] lends itself to self-parody and modification perhaps more than any other genre' Shklovsky described such digressions as a way of introducing 'a variety of critical and philosophical materials' into a familiar work through having the main characters momentarily replaced by random storytellers. 'Toying with the reader's impatience, the author repeatedly reminds him of the deserted hero. Nonetheless, he does not return to him after the digression, and reminding the reader serves only to renew the reader's expectation.'[163] And so, even when the double-banked digression that is *Love & Monsters* has fulfilled its purpose of filling a production slot, we're still listening to Elton by the episode's end, instead of finding ourselves safely back inside the TARDIS console room.

According to Shklovsky, anything an audience has gotten accustomed

---

isolated from their interrelationship in reality, affect each other only in accordance with the laws of the given artistic nexus.' Shklovsky, *Theory of Prose*, p19.
[163] Shklovsky, *Theory of Prose*, p192.

to – whether in stories or in real life – can be stripped of its accrued connotations and looked at with a fresh pair of eyes. This applies to anything we're ever asked to accept as normal: for example, the plot of a story, the decisions made by a hero, the laws of our land, the relationships we have with the people around us, and the circumstances we put up with in our lives. Ostrannenye doesn't mean that the things themselves **become** strange; instead, it means that familiar things are shown from unexpected, yet mundane perspectives, which then relieve those things of uncritical familiarity and show us how strange they **already are**. (Or as Douglas Adams once wrote, 'more differed from than differing'[164]). The examined element 'changes its form without changing its essence'[165] and in achieving this, ostrannenye can make storytelling into 'a road in which the foot feels acutely the stones beneath it'[166]. In short, Shklovsky celebrated stories which ask us to question all the things we wouldn't think to question.

Of course, that entire process is already at the heart of **Doctor Who**. In any given situation, the Doctor can serve as the new perspective that makes our everyday lives look marvellously weird. It's part of what makes the character so exciting and affirming, and he tells us as much in *Father's Day*: 'Street corner, two in the morning, getting a taxi home. I've never had a life like that.' Everything we do in our tiny human lives is strange to such a protagonist. And when we're with the Doctor, looking through his/her eyes, we can treat the circumstances around us from a totally alien point of view – literally

---

[164] Adams, Douglas, *The Restaurant at the End of the Universe*, p245.
[165] Shklovsky, *Theory of Prose*, p6.
[166] Shklovsky, *Theory of Prose*, p15.

alienating our own world. Such a way of seeing is in fact part of all sci-fi. The genre as a whole opens up the idea that our everyday circumstances are not the only way of life out there and, therefore, can be interrogated and altered. Every vision of different times and spaces signals that we have the power to change our own reality.

But TARDIS life soon lost some of this estranging power. As early as *The Web Planet* (1965), the TARDIS console room became emphasised as a cosy and familiar environment in contrast to alien worlds. An 'unusually large number of scenes set inside the ship' were included deliberately to make the planet Vortis look more alien in comparison, since 'what had been an alien control room in **Doctor Who**'s earliest days [was] now a familiar, safe, even homely setting after fifteen months and twelve serials'[167]. Shklovsky described this exact effect, examining how a deviation from the norm may in turn become normal, and may become a yardstick for further deviations; in which case a return to the norm (e.g. to the everyday) will eventually seem strange[168].

This is why Shklovsky preferred the new angle to be an everyday, sober, bare-bones perspective. An estranging story can describe 'the exotic against the touching though feebly expressed background' of the 'everyday life' of ordinary people, 'enabling the reader to reassemble it once again'[169]. The realism of the new viewpoint makes it come across as much more accessible and plausible to the audience. The lack of definition or complexity in the new point-of-

---

[167] Wiggins, Martin, *The Web Planet* DVD info text.
[168] Shklovsky, *Theory of Prose*, p21, citing theories by language scholar Broder Christiansen.
[169] Shklovsky, *Theory of Prose*, p 209.

view character, e.g. the blankness of Elton's everyday life, allows the focus to stay on the thing which is being estranged, rather than distracting the reader with full immersion into the new pair of eyes. And a disjointed, unreliable or ambiguous narration serves to make the reader think critically about what's being described.

Shklovsky's examples of ostrannenye include the laws of land ownership shown from the naïve perspective of a horse, as seen in Tolstoy; as well as taboo erotic acts alluded to with silly, cheeky metaphors[170]. When access to all of time and space is shown from the naïve perspective of LINDA, and queerness is symbolised with something as silly as a paving slab, these effects are in full force. And while the Doctor can invite us to look at our everyday circumstances afresh, only a character as normal as Elton can in turn snap us back, flip us over and ask us to look at the Doctor's life critically through regular human eyes – to re-estrange our now-familiar alien hero by returning to the earthbound norm.

The attitude which Shklovsky, Brecht and Davies have in common is their enthusiastic embracing of kitsch, mundanity and everyday experiences in art. They've all celebrated jarring language and unexpected perspectives, which drag audiences down from purely immersive drama and remind them just how ridiculous things are. A narrator like Elton interrupting the action to say 'it is going to get scaaaaaary!' conveys that **Doctor Who**'s usual dramatic tension doesn't apply here. The same goes for a horrifying absorption followed by the absorbed character getting stuck on someone's arse. And when the monster chases Elton in broad daylight, we can find ourselves made aware of our own scepticism, much the same as

---

[170] Shklovsky, *Theory of Prose*, p7.

when a Brecht performance suddenly turns on the bright lights over the audience to enforce emotional distance from the plot.

This rollercoaster effect – the fiction being immersive one moment, and too silly for immersion the next – can be seen as a game between the writer and the audience. Such a game slots into the interplay between comedy and horror, or between comedy and tragedy. But it's even more delicate; this way of writing can invite the audience to roll their eyes and to **question the choices of the author**. The author and the audience become intensely vulnerable to each other, with the fiction caught in the middle, so to speak.

Here we can see another level of metafictionality, on top of all the fandom symbolism. It's another way for the episode to cast us out of the immersive fiction and to make us consider our real-life circumstances. We watch the show to see the Doctor, and not only is said hero out of our reach for the majority of the story, but we're also constantly made aware of our own real-life fandom circles **and** of Russell T Davies himself as the real person serving us these bathetic scenes. The experience is designed to be frustrating, and only becomes less so if we agree to participate in this little game and to play by Davies' rules. We can end up feeling as if the showrunner is holding our typical enjoyment of the series hostage – as if he's telling us that we won't be getting it back until we've submitted to his whims.

'Especially the Usual!'

Bertolt Brecht's methods were similar to the ones that his Russian contemporary Shklovsky described. But where Shklovsky was mainly concerned with theory, Brecht wanted to use his art to change the world.

The German playwright employed radical shifts in format that went against everything theatre-goers were used to. For one of his plays, he covered the theatre walls in posters showing, in huge letters, the words 'STOP GAWKING SO ROMANTICALLY'[171]. Every part of his writing was calculated to tear his fans away from their accustomed perspectives. He felt that unless society's circumstances were questioned, they could 'quickly and inadvertently acquire great independence and the appearance of great unchangeability' as though 'they can't be stopped', and that the inclusion of familiar social dynamics in a story 'can only truly influence an audience when it is countered.'[172] In other words, when Brecht presented things in estranged ways, his goal was to make his spectators question the supposed sociopolitical unchangeability of the world around them. He countered the idea that **familiar** things are **normal** things. By alienating audiences from his stories, he meant for them to subsequently stop treating their own societies as normal, and to start changing everything.

To this end, his naïve figures frequently address the viewers directly and – like Elton – discuss the injustices and mysteries around them. And like Elton, they ramble on in a resigned way without exploring any workable solution. Brecht encouraged his audiences to step back from the immersive lure of fiction this way, and to think for themselves instead – specifically, to come up with real-life solutions

---

[171] Brecht, Bertolt, 'Zu *Trommeln in der Nacht*' ['On "Drums in the Night"'] in *Schriften 4*, p14.
[172] Brecht, Bertolt, 'Lehre von eingreifenden Sätzen (praktikablen Definitionen)' ['Teachings of engaging Sentences (feasible Definitions)'] in Hecht, Werner et al, eds, *Bertolt Brecht: Schriften 1* ['Writings 1'], p524.

where these figures stop short[173].

Much like in *Love & Monsters* and in the ostrannenye effect that Shklovsky discussed, Brecht showed his audiences worlds of ordinary people, living unlucky lives and walking down utterly normal streets. His figures offered recognisable viewpoints which, precisely because of their mundanity, were able to provide a sober perspective and question everything his audiences had become accustomed to.

Like Davies, Brecht also described how comedy and serious drama can lift each other up. He liked to draw in his audiences with humour, before punching them in the gut with scathing social criticism. The soap opera vibe seen in Jackie's home life (and in Davies' early TV work) isn't far off Brecht's style either – the German playwright similarly invited his fans into the mundane kitsch of working-class family life. Shouty mums and schmaltzy, dysfunctional romances formed the beating heart of his plays. He wanted his viewers to be unsatisfied with all the bathetic and melodramatic story elements and, in their dissatisfaction, to reflect critically on everything that was unsatisfying in their real-life circumstances too[174].

Brecht summarised this goal for his audiences in 1938 as: 'Look with distrust! Question necessity. Especially the usual! [...] Don't think of life's constants as natural! [...] so that nothing should become unchangeable.'[175] This kind of distrust evoked by writers can also

---

[173] Brecht, 'Couragemodell 1949', p241.
[174] Brecht, Bertolt, 'Über experimentelles Theater' ['On Experimental Theatre'] in *Schriften 2*, p547.
[175] Brecht, Bertolt, *Die Ausnahme und die Regel* ['The Exception and the Rule'] in Hecht, Werner et al, eds, *Bertolt Brecht: Stücke 3* ['Plays 3'], p237.

provide whole new insights into things like, say, a decades-old television show's narrative structure and the actions of said show's protagonists. It allows viewers to judge the show because it gives them **space** to judge, away from the Doctor's vicinity and the familiar embrace of the TARDIS. And a fictional environment that encourages investigative distrust, like a London Investigation 'N' Detective Agency, helps fans to take that step. As mentioned in Chapter 2, the way the LINDA members form receptive audiences for each other's fan works and analyses constantly reminds viewers of their own investigative real-life position as audiences.

The contradictions in Brecht's works symbolise the kinds of social contradictions people face in everyday life; for example, how people just like LINDA choose to work in humiliating circumstances under men just like Kennedy, because he allows them better access to the things they want and need. Brecht wanted to show how absurd this is. A similar sense of absurdity is exposed by Stoppard's Guildenstern when, doomed to accept the machinations of the larger plot enveloping him and Rosencrantz, he mutters how 'There must have been a moment at the beginning, where we could have said no'. It's a common theme in stories of this genre: the realisation that there are ways to escape from the proscribed narrative, that there are other choices to be made. With Elton's big 'I'm sorry, Victor, but you're on your own because I am leaving!' moment, we see a breaking point and realise there's another option – that of resisting exploitative authority.

Love & Monsters echoes Brecht's notion that in a court of law, it would be advisable to call in judges from far-away lands, who would see our own culture's habits as strange and even unnecessary. On this topic Brecht wrote: 'Injustice often gains the character of justice simply because it happens often. The newcomers let themselves be told everything as new, enabling them to notice what's conspicuous'[176]. LINDA are a bit like these judges, seeing the Doctor from a wholly different frame of reference and finding just about everything they see in him unusual. Placed among them, viewers can shift their own judgment of the Doctor as well.

LINDA show us the Doctor through the eyes of people who are scared of him, and in awe, and just plain confused as to why he's part of their lives. (As are we since, aside from Elton, none of them explain how they first learned of the Doctor.) Their viewpoints show us just how strange **Doctor Who**'s premise truly is – how utterly alien, as soon as we take a step back.

Much like Brecht's figures, LINDA are not complete people with daily lives or detailed personal histories that audiences can fully immerse themselves in. Instead, they're examples of specific types of social **actions** we may encounter in our own circles[177]. The writing presents them as archetypes rather than detailed individuals. Even the name LINDA itself, recycled from Davies' previous project **Why Don't You ...?**, lacks individuality[178].

We know practically nothing about Bliss aside from how she symbolises fan artists, as she has only nine lines in the entire episode. We learn nothing of Mr Skinner outside of the brief scene that tells us he's a writer. As in Brecht's stories, these figures are malleable

---

[176] Brecht, Bertolt, 'Rechtsprechung' ['Jurisdiction'], in Knopf, Jan et al, eds, *Bertolt Brecht: Prosa 3* ['Prose 3'], p444.
[177] Brecht, Bertolt, 'Dialektische Kritik' ['Dialectical Criticism'] in *Schriften 1*, p520.
[178] *The Complete History* #53, p53.

models that fans can project people from their own reality onto[179]. They click for us not through any kind of complex inner lives, but through the way they spark recognition and put us in mind of our real circumstances.

This type of character building is reminiscent of what literary scholar Itō Gō calls 'kyara' (キャラ, half of the Japanese pronunciation of 'character' – 'kyarakutaa' – and thereby meaning 'half a character'). Kyara are instantly recognisable archetypes. Itō describes them as proto-characters with quasi-personalities like 'a bunch of strokes drawn on paper'[180]. They settle easily into a narrative by virtue of being plain and pared-down. In essence, they're blank paper dolls in highly familiar shapes which can be given more intricate narrative roles with the right clothes, haircuts and speech balloons depending on the fiction they're put into. Such characters can be visual silhouettes, emotional stereotypes and collections of traits; the classic doll Barbie, who can be given any job or narrative with a simple change of wardrobe, is one example. The archetypes around talking animals in fables (sly Mr Fox, loyal Dog, or wise old Owl) are another, fleshed out as little or as much as the story requires but already recognisable in our cultures from the moment they appear.

This is at the core of why we recognise LINDA so easily as our fellow fans, no matter how sparse their dialogue is or how stripped-down they are in personality and appearance. For example, Bliss is like a kyara of 'sweet, artsy hippie' flavoured with a handful of additional

---

[179] Brecht, Bertolt, 'Der Dreigroschenprozess' ['The Threepenny Process'] in *Schriften 1*, p464.
[180] Itō, Gō, *TEZUKA is Dead: Postmodernist and Modernist Approaches to Japanese Manga*, pp 107-113.

character elements. Audiences are aware of her type's existence on a conceptual level long before they first see *Love & Monsters*, and are instantly able to ascribe a personality to her by the way she hooks into basic reference frames. The effect is even stronger with Elton's mother, whose inviting appearance of kindness and archetypical femininity make her iconic in the same way as Itō's kyara. She's a blank, but a blank that evokes instant recognition in the audience.

Davies confirms that this process is deliberate on his part, in describing his vision of the Bowie Base One crew in *The Waters of Mars*: 'They have to be [...] distinctive, simple, archetypal, to make me care about them, but quickly. It sounds like a contradiction, but it isn't.'[181] LINDA can be described the same way. **Doctor Who** is 'designed to incorporate likeable characters,' Davies states, 'because so much else is going on. You're creating monsters, plots, worlds, environments, so even fairly complicated characters like Rose are sketches, in a sense, to be filled in by good acting. A likeable character is shorthand, to get you into the story, fast.'[182] Part of this is, as he reminds us, due to 'the speed with which you have to introduce any supporting character in **Doctor Who**, given that they're components of a much bigger, much odder format'[183] – but it can be argued that LINDA's tiny selves also perfectly showcase just how much bigger, odder, darker, madder and better the world around them is, both within their story and beyond the limits of the fourth wall.

The strength of such brush-stroke kyara lies in their universality and

---

[181] Davies and Cook, *The Writer's Tale*, p428.
[182] Davies and Cook, *The Writer's Tale*, p40.
[183] Davies and Cook, *The Writer's Tale*, p121.

robustness, in their ability to keep on existing with or without a narrative crafted around them. Even through the LINDA members practically vanish from **Doctor Who** again when the credits roll, the kyara archetypes that lie at their foundation continue to exist in our minds as we see them reflected in people all across our fandom. Whatever we take away from *Love & Monsters* can end up reverberating in the way we subsequently see and treat these real-life people we encounter.

The critical process that's enabled by all these little narrative tricks can extend beyond the Doctor as a person and to **Doctor Who** as a franchise. If characters like Elton were to show up more often, bringing their own cameras or story-crafting into our idea of what **Doctor Who** actually **is**, we might end up questioning the very fabric of the show. This could lead to TV episodes subverting the structure on an even deeper level (an idea prodded at in 2015's *Sleep No More*) or engaging in dialogue with the audience in ways a typical space adventure would never allow. This way, we might even be encouraged by the show itself to re-examine our own fannish loyalty to its more unfortunate aspects – those bits that are discriminatory, nonsensical, or just plain bad – without the supposed 'right' moral of the story being handed to us on a platter and affirmed by our heroes.

Perhaps Your Most Infuriatingly Human Trait

Cultural scholar Joshua Vasquez states in his essay 'The Moral Economy of **Doctor Who**: Forgiving Fans and the Objects of Their Devotion' that fans can 'engage in a kind of love affair' with their favourite things. This love can make them oblivious to the less fortunate parts of a work, through 'a kind of **forgiveness** which occurs between fans and the objects of their fandom in which the fan forgives those objects for their transgressions or **missteps**'. The creators of the fiction can, deliberately or accidentally, 'program that forgiveness within the fan'[184].

Vasquez emphasises that '[f]ans accept this image of the Doctor as always fighting for justice and equality, always on the side of the downtrodden and always against those forces that represent cruelty, oppression and tyranny, because the program instilled the truth of that characterization within them'[185]. This extends, Vasquez states, to fans subsequently seeing **the show itself** as heroic and fundamentally just, and using that axiomatic idea to handwave away its less graceful moments such as racism, sexism or the harmful misrepresentation of real-life events. In doing so, they can sustain their devotion to the franchise guilt-free.

Fans may see this as a sort of trade-off: when many aspects are good, the sociopolitically iffy aspects may then not 'count' in their eyes. That way, fans can continue to enjoy the work without having to confront its problems. Fan social identity is linked to media that are consumed, and consequently any attack on the media can feel like

---

[184] Vasquez, Joshua, 'The Moral Economy of **Doctor Who**: Forgiving Fans and the Objects of Their Devotion' in *Ruminations, Peregrinations, and Regenerations*, p234. Emphasis in original. In the interest of providing more than one perspective: fan studies scholar Matt Hills gives a rebuttal in his essay '"Proper Distance" in the Ethical Positioning of Scholar-Fandoms: Between Academics' and Fans' Moral Economies?' published in *Fan Culture: Theory/Practice*, in which he calls Vasquez out for assuming a normative position in his scholarly identity and for portraying fans' attitudes as overly uncritical and homogeneous.

[185] Vasquez, 'The Moral Economy of Doctor Who', p242.

an attack on the self. There's a deep-seated hunger for interacting with works which can be shown off as flawless, and of which every aspect could reflect positively on the devoted audience.

For many fans, any blemish on that ideal can result in either refusal to address the bad bits or, conversely, in feeling that one must uncouple the fandom from one's identity and denounce the now-othered work of art (plus any fans who merrily continue to hang on) as tainted, irredeemable and forever 'gross'. The art of acknowledging that compassionate and discriminatory aspects can exist in the same works without cancelling each other out can be difficult for fandoms to navigate.

In his treatment of this topic, Vasquez draws on the work of Henry Jenkins, who first coined the concept of a 'moral economy'. Such a symbolic economy consists of social norms in fandom which 'enable the fan to navigate the line between challenging the text of their devotion, especially when it is perceived as straying from expectations, and remaining loyal to that text's structures'[186]. In other words: sometimes we fail to question uncomfortable bits because we want to continue loving the fiction and being part of the fannish in-group. A wilful ignorance can be used as currency to stay engaged with the fandom.

Which is where unusually-structured episodes with unexpected perspectives, like *Love & Monsters*, come in. These can help us to break out of that mindset, and to address the good, the bad and the ugly in our favourite show from whole new points of view. The

---

[186] Vasquez, 'The Moral Economy of Doctor Who', pp234-235, drawing on Henry Jenkins.

nastiness hiding behind all the space adventure glitz and glamour gets exposed and proffered up in the bright light of day.

This is especially interesting when it comes to the 10th Doctor. All incarnations of the Time Lord fall somewhere along the sliding scale of hero versus anti-hero – while the Doctor as embodied by Peter Davison was heroic to a fault and could typically be counted on to do the right thing, the incarnations played by Sylvester McCoy, John Hurt and Peter Capaldi, for example, emphasised their moral ambiguity. It can be argued that the 10th Doctor is duplicitous, in that he takes all the morally questionable actions of an anti-hero while sauntering about as though he's a hero through and through. He considers himself justified in anything he chooses to do. Simply put, if we call the mainly-heroic Doctors 'Type A' and the more anti-heroic Doctors 'Type B', the 10th Doctor is a Type B wearing the mask of a Type A. And quite possibly not even aware of it[187]. A similar attitude was seen in the 20th century Doctors at times, but the show in those days simply didn't focus much on its protagonist's inner emotional life. Under Davies, these layers of storytelling and their effect on the Doctor's own sense of self were finally addressed on television.

Going back a moment to the idea of power among **Doctor Who** writers, the idea of the renegade offers more perspective here. As the vagrant who once left his aristocratic homeworld, the Doctor has consistently been portrayed as someone who flouts the rules and tells authority figures to shove it. The Doctor rails against convention and against the power granted to the upper classes of the universe, making up new rules and more progressive ways of life that benefit the common people instead. The sonic screwdriver is the ultimate

---

[187] Credit goes to my friend Charles Whitt for this line of thought.

symbol of this attitude: a tool associated with the working class, which can be used to gain access anywhere, anytime, regardless of where those in power mark their territory as inaccessible to the masses.

It could be said that all of **Doctor Who**, and indeed all of sci-fi, is about trespassing. Characters and audiences enter spaces together that would otherwise be inaccessible to people of their location, social class or era. Seen in this context, Elton's exclusion from the TARDIS throughout *Love & Monsters* feels uncomfortable not just because we want our regular hero back, but also because Elton's lack of access is fundamentally opposed to the premise of the show and to the sci-fi genre as a whole. And we can pity Elton, stuck at home talking to his camcorder – because after we leave *Love & Monsters* behind, **we** can go right back to accompanying the Doctor throughout all of time and space.

It's interesting to spot parallels between the Doctor gaining access to closed-off territory and all the fan-creators steadily gaining access to the lore that the BBC claims power over, or simply leaving the **Who** homeworld (so to speak) and forging their own paths in spinoffs and partially-licensed works and charity publications. In a sense, every fan who creates part of **Doctor Who**'s sprawling mythology can feel as if they're following in the Doctor's footsteps, entering other people's spaces on one's own terms.

But at the same time, the Doctor is still the ultimate authority figure – a pompous Lord of temporal continuity, curating the universe from his/her police box and didactically playing judge, jury and executioner all across the timelines. And seen in such a light, that same sonic screwdriver which allows access anywhere, any time takes on very different connotations.

As John Cordone and Michelle Cordone point out in their essay 'Who Is the Doctor?; The Meta-Narrative of **Doctor Who**', the Doctor is still an aristocrat by heritage and by bearing, and therefore a mirror of English feudal lordship. If different times can be travelled to as easily as foreign countries, then being a Lord of Time carries the same kind of social advantage as being a lord of land. The traditional land ownership associated with feudal power (and derided in Marxist discourse) potentially becomes the Doctor's access to all of time and space in the show's narrative. And this attitude of 'I'm allowed anywhere!'[188] isn't just a roguish anti-authoritarian quirk, but can simultaneously **also** be an assertion of authority, of gerontocracy, and of innate qualities that are presented as superior to those of all the common humans. To quote the Cordones: 'This sense of entitlement is often read as simple non-conformity' but 'as a lord, the Doctor does not need to conform to the rules and regulations of those beneath his station.'[189] One notably explicit TV acknowledgement and subversion of the Doctor's invasive trespassing in this manner came in 2018's *Arachnids in the UK* when, about to sonic open someone's front door, she stops to ask if it would be 'appropriate'.

Even if we see the Doctor as a self-made innovator, as someone fighting 'the man' of Time Lord society by reshaping the universe in defiance of their laws, it's important to acknowledge that our hero

---

[188] *The Five Doctors* (1983).
[189] Cordone, Michelle and John Cordone, 'Who is the Doctor? The Meta-Narrative of **Doctor Who**' in *Ruminations, Peregrinations, and Regenerations*, p11.

isn't just a rebel tinkering away in a little blue tool shed – but someone with actual, impactful control over the lives of others, who imposes personal values on worlds that he/she chooses to stay an outsider to. The Doctor is able to socially engineer a temporary sense of access and belonging and thereby consistently gain control over other people's spaces. Which can be a very positive thing for outcasts to achieve; but at the same time a very dangerous thing for those in power to claim as their right.

Being part of a fandom is deeply tied in with the ideas of access and belonging. Henry Jenkins even characterises fandom itself as those who 'trespass upon others' property; they grab it and hold onto it; they internalize its meaning and remake these borrowed terms'[190]. But what does this mean when the self and the property of others become merged; when the fans are also the creators; and when the creators then try to make audiences see them as fans, by depicting those same fans within the fan-creator work as trespassers?

Fittingly, the way people gain entry into each other's spaces is a thread seen in *Love & Monsters* on multiple levels. LINDA try to gain access to the Doctor's world; the Doctor is seen in Elton's living room uninvited; Elton has difficulty moving inside his own house after the Sycorax invasion breaches his window; Elton plans his infiltration into Jackie's home life; and the Abzorbaloff invades the group's social and physical spaces in increasingly gruesome ways – all the way down to consuming their bodies.

The way we interpret the unasked-for crossing of such boundaries depends on whose perspective we're seeing the story from. When

---

[190] Jenkins, *Textual Poachers*, p116.

we're on the side of the Doctor, the invasion of personal space and private territory as performed by the TARDIS crew often seems fun and adventurous; but when the Doctor is seen through another pair of eyes, these same breaches can take on a much more sinister tone. This coding is not unlike the classic 'invasive foreign monster' trope discussed in chapter 4, but with the twist of the foreign outsider also being our hero, **as well as** a Lord of time and space in general. The Doctor's pride in being a disruptive influence can blinker both him/her and the audience to the notion that such an influence can be unwanted. And when trespassing into someone's space is paired with flouting their rules, dismissing their social conventions and altering their culture's history, that's not always just the inspirational journeys of a quirky vagrant – it can also be plain old colonising.

And so, the Doctor is ultimately both things at once: the renegade and the ruler; the commoner and the aristo; the refugee and the tourist; the defender and the invader; the downtrodden and the dictator. The Doctor always **personally** embodies the dichotomy between seeing the universe vs. owning it – an authoritarian Lord masked as a hapless traveller, slumming across history.

We can recognise Victor Kennedy as a fake oligarch who's actually just a hungry bloke. We can see LINDA as the struggling masses who can gain control by becoming content creators on their own terms. We can see such aspects as echoes of Davies, if we like. But the role of the Doctor as a bridge between contradictory extremes is the most fascinating one of all. Because if LINDA and the Abzorbaloff stand in for **Doctor Who** fans in the metafictional narrative of this episode, then the Doctor here can stand in for **Doctor Who** as a TV show – and consequently also for those people in charge of the series, specifically the BBC and Davies. The power that the Time Lord holds over others provides fascinating parallels to the power that creators hold over their stories.

In presenting himself as a regular fan while also simultaneously lording over the TV series, Davies displays a pattern similar to that seen in the Doctor – that of someone who can assert authority, and take the people around him on wild rides that may not at all go where they want, but who then still expects to walk among the masses and pass for one of us. If the Doctor's attitude towards Elton in this episode seems inscrutable and leaves us wondering what game he thinks he's playing, the same can be said of Davies' attitude towards us as viewers, as he cuts us off from our usual perspective and forces us to play along.

Powers of 10

Returning to the 10th Doctor in a less symbolic sense, the interplay between his compassionate and authoritative sides is a defining part of his character. As the series arcs progressed and his morally questionable actions continued to be cloaked by his kind smile and his bravado, this incarnation of the Doctor became someone who **needed** to be called out. Davies talks lovingly about how the 'dark side to David's Doctor' shines through: 'It's subtle and, because of that, so powerful. [...] It's magnificent. Terrifying!'[191]

Of course, since the narrative held off on the grand epiphany moment until *The Waters of Mars*, any perspective that *Love & Monsters* could provide was just one small part of the larger picture. (Which isn't to suggest that Elton's adventure was deliberate buildup to the specific dénouement in *The Waters of Mars* – which was

---

[191] Davies and Cook, *The Writer's Tale*, p379.

decided only months before broadcast[192] – but rather that all these episodes mutually influence each other's meaning.) The Doctor's actions in *The Waters of Mars* would become a culmination of how this Doctor turns his back on the world when it suits him. Our hero's callous, inscrutable treatment of Elton in *Love & Monsters* is a step on the way to that point.

The Doctor seen from LINDA's perspective can seem monstrous, thoroughly alien and worthy of critical judgment – but there are too many unknowns, too many blanks to fill in for us to draw any direct conclusions. *Love & Monsters* was never the finish line in showing us the 10th Doctor's shadow side. It didn't present us with a clear direction to go in, or a specific type of judgment to impose. Rather, it was an invitation to simply walk a mile in the shoes of someone affected by the Doctor's actions. It gave viewers a light bulb and a lampshade, rather than a neon sign.

On top of that, while the Doctor seems neutral towards them in this episode, Moffat's later minisode 'Time Crash' (2007) has the fifth incarnation of the Doctor talking about 'that LINDA lot' with disdain. This retroactively contextualises the group as gadflies, people who were already annoying the Doctor six bodies before he grew the Tennant face. Where Elton was initially meant to have lived through the story of 20th century **Who** in *Love & Monsters*' first drafts, 'Time Crash' reverses this effect as it turns out that the 20th century Doctor actually lived through the story of LINDA. This further includes LINDA in **Doctor Who**, but it can **also** mean that LINDA is even more excluded from the narrative than previously thought, since their outsider status goes back throughout the series' decades of

---

[192] Davies and Cook, *The Writer's Tale*, p571.

adventures. Additionally, by comparing his very fannish future self – embodied by actual squeeing fanboy Tennant – to LINDA, the fifth Doctor signals just how arbitrary the distinction between fans and creators really is.

Love & Monsters leaves its impact on the series' structure, but perhaps not so much on the Doctor as a character just yet. It's two series later, in *Journey's End*, that Davies finally provides evidence of the Doctor having mourned LINDA at all. When Davros calls the Doctor out on the carnage he leaves in his wake, flashes are shown of those who have died by being associated with him. These include brief visuals of LINDA members, presumably to show the Doctor's distress over the effect that he's had on them. But if LINDA ever had any other impact on the hero, the audience never finds out. The little group of geeks are a minor nuisance, at most, in the Doctor's very long life.

So let's turn back to Elton. Even though he never really confronts the Doctor to his face, the way Amy and Rory would later do, his musings after the adventure's end are still an act of criticism. He talks about how his new friends have ended up destroyed, and how 'maybe that's what happens if you touch the Doctor, even for a second'. It's a powerful statement (even if it's obviously exaggerated) precisely because the Doctor isn't there to distract us or talk over it. For once, he doesn't get the final word. And that is exceedingly rare in televised **Doctor Who**. If the Doctor has any response at all to Elton's accusations, it's in his self-description to the Abzorbaloff a few scenes earlier: 'Sweet – yeah. Passionate – maybe. But don't ever mistake that for nice.' An unintentional confirmation of Elton's experiences, rather than a rebuttal.

Still, Elton too is susceptible to the moral economy of his obsession. He and the rest of LINDA could probably work out that the Abzorbaloff is behind their friends' disappearances, but they use their wilful ignorance as currency to stay engaged with the symbolic fandom and to gain access to materials. Where Jackie has found herself becoming 'hard', Elton chooses acceptance. His line 'It's not his fault' in describing the Doctor echoes the sentiments of fans throughout history, who are quick to forgive a creator's awkward moments simply because they love the fiction. 'Turns out I've had the most terrible things happen', he says. 'And the most brilliant things. And sometimes, well, I can't tell the difference'.

Davies states that **Doctor Who** fans are 'very good at swallowing stuff and kind of getting on with it' to keep up their devotion to the franchise[193]. When we – like Elton – face a rude awakening about the object of our fascination, something that draws everything we thought we knew into question, we may find ourselves – like Elton – still lumping the bad in with the good and simply telling ourselves that it's okay. We – like Elton – know that the Doctor can be rude, and awful, and can leave behind a trail of death... but in the end, those terrible things can be the most brilliant things to us, too. And sometimes we don't even **want** to tell the difference.

In a Brechtian sense, we can interpret this as an invitation to stay critical where Elton is more inclined to forgive – to continue where the characters leave off. Conversely, maybe the writing here invites us to be lenient towards this Doctor's flaws, so that later explorations of his dark side are more likely to blindside us for dramatic effect. Or, well, maybe Elton is a regular guy with regular feelings who's pretty

---

[193] **Toby Hadoke's Who's Round #59.**

much just winging it.

Of course, this episode is also just part of a big entertainment show that needs to market its twists and turns. The ending scene serves a much more practical narrative purpose as well: that of foreshadowing the series finale. 'I keep thinking of Rose and Jackie', Elton says. 'And how much longer before they pay the price.' It's a neat little prelude for the story arcs to come, in which both women would end up stranded in a parallel universe, utterly cut off from the Doctor's life. What Elton doesn't realise is how much he'll have in common with them in the years to follow: they become outsiders to the TARDIS world, irrevocably changed by the Doctor's travels, and cast out from the TV show altogether.

CHAPTER 7: 'WHAT HE NEVER WON'T REPRESENT'
Encoding and Decoding Media

Tell me, reader... am I a good fan?

What **is** a good fan? Someone who interprets a work of art just the way the creator intended? Or someone who resculpts it into something new?

Before diving into this topic, I'd like to take a moment to quote **Doctor Who** archivist and historian Andrew Pixley on the fans he feels he belongs with – those:

> 'who aren't content to sit back and take from others, but have been to dusty archives and wind-swept quarries pursuing that elusive piece in the jigsaw that helps us form a complete picture of what did go on behind the scenes of our favourite show. And so we work together. And as a team, we can achieve things we never believed possible, lending our own areas of expertise to each other's projects and making each other's work more comprehensive.'[194]

And isn't that all of LINDA? Isn't that so many of us too? If you're reading this book, chances are you're not satisfied with just taking **Doctor Who** at face value. You probably want to dive in a little, poke it, look at it from different angles and see what's hidden inside. Luckily, there are endless ways to do so.

---

[194] Pixley, Andrew, 'Hidden Treasure: The Compulsion to Research **Doctor Who**'.

One of the most famous theories of media interpretation comes from literary theorist and Marxist aesthetician Roland Barthes. His 1967 essay 'The Death of the Author' gave the perspective that the creator ultimately isn't in charge of the creation's meaning. Instead, Barthes theorised that meaning is formed only once the audience receives a work of art and interprets it. This is linked to the idea that no creator can ever be fully aware of their influences and of their subconscious drive to create certain kinds of content – so that a text is 'a woven fabric'[195] based on 'innumerable centres of culture'[196] rather than on one individual experience. Such a model makes the author into a funnel, guiding existing concepts through art into the reader's consciousness.

Echoes of **Doctor Who**'s collaborative, tapestry-like lore-building can be seen in Barthes' description of how 'a text is made of multiple writings, drawn from many cultures and entering into mutual relations of dialogue, parody, contestation'. Taking Brecht's alienation theory and transforming it into the idea of deliberately alienating text and author from each other, Barthes stated that 'a text's unity lies not in its origins but in its destination'. The author's personality becomes irrelevant to the work's contents. In this 'truly revolutionary' model, the audience (and therefore the fan) rather than the creator is granted dialectical power to give meaning to every story[197].

---

[195] Barthes, Roland, 'From Work to Text' in Heath, Stephen, trans/ed, *Image, Music, Text*, p159.
[196] Barthes, Roland, 'The Death of the Author' in *Image, Music, Text*, p146.
[197] Barthes, 'The Death of the Author', pp147-8.

Shklovsky had touched on similar ideas decades before. He stated that 'a work of art is perceived against a background of and by association with other works of art. The form of a work of art is determined by its relationship with other pre-existing forms. [...] All works of art [...] are created either as a parallel or an antithesis to some model. The new form makes its appearance not in order to express a new content, but rather, to replace an old form that has already outlived its artistic usefulness.'[198] Like Barthes, he emphasised that no creation exists in a vacuum and that all art is part of the larger culture that it's created in, to be continuously re-written and re-interpreted in an ever-shifting process.

But authorial intent, not to mention the cults of personality that can form around creators, can also be seen as an integral part of a text. Cultural studies scholar Stuart Hall explored this more multifaceted idea in his 1973 theory of encoding and decoding. He described media as 'polysemic' – that is, containing different meanings for different creators, distributors, reproducers and audiences[199]. In response to Barthes' model, Hall stated that the cultural influences, the work of art itself, the creators, the distribution methods and the audience all contribute to interpretation. In his view, what the audience experiences from a work of art (like, say, a television episode) isn't just a one-on-one transmission of the production team's intentions, but a communication process based on shared understanding.

---

[198] Shklovsky, *Theory of Prose*, p20. Original italics removed to improve legibility.

[199] Hall, Stuart, 'Encoding, decoding' in During, Simon, ed, *The Cultural Studies Reader*, p98.

The encoders (for example, the author and the distributor) have their intentions and particular frames of reference; the decoders (e.g. the audience) have their own perspectives, most likely different. These groups can also overlap, as a distributor or any other intermediary party needs to both encode and decode. Because of this, the dominant-hegemonic position (the common and/or intended interpretation) is just one of countless decoding options. Certain combinations of symbols that make sense to an audience – words, images, sounds – can contribute to a story being interpreted as intended, but this is never a guarantee[200].

Building on Marx's economic theories, Hall argued that consumption is a necessary part of media communication, and that consumption itself is therefore an **aspect** of the means of cultural production[201]. Even purely receptive consumption of only the hegemonic, intended message (which 'carries with it the stamp of legitimacy'[202]) still makes audiences inherently part of the production process. But the true power of fans, Hall theorised, lies in their ability to respond to the text. He also linked this to Marxist ideas: when television viewers opt for negotiated decoding, in which they disagree with the encoded message and 'make their own ground rules' in response, the transformative power of fandom can mimic the revolutionary actions of workers as they revolt against the dominant classes[203].

---

[200] Hall, 'Encoding, decoding', p99.
[201] For a scathingly critical perspective on how the discourse 'deals with the taint of fan consumption by recuperating fan-consumers as "producers" and "creators"' through this sort of goalpost moving, see Hills, *Fan Cultures*, p52ff.
[202] Hall, 'Encoding, decoding', p102.
[203] Hall, 'Encoding, decoding', p102.

Jenkins and other scholars nowadays increasingly propose treating Hall's model as a stepping stone towards an even more fluid line of thinking, in which media reception doesn't **need** to be categorised as receptive or resistant, as hegemonic or as countercultural – but can simply be a continuous dialogue[204].

This corner of media theory seems to resonate with Davies. The showrunner plans out specific emotions to evoke in **Doctor Who**'s audience, and he deliberately positions himself as an auteur in the public eye[205], but he agrees that it's still not his place to force any response on fans[206]. He values the agency of audiences to reach whatever conclusion makes the most sense to them[207]. This sentiment is echoed in LINDA's fannish interpretations of the Doctor, which are abstract, overwrought and highly dubious, but which are still celebrated in Davies' writing as creative expressions of decoding.

But as Jenkins counters, 'controlling the means of cultural reception, while an important step, does not provide an adequate substitute for access to the means of cultural production and distribution'[208].

---

[204] Jenkins, *Textual Poachers*, pages 88ff, building critically on De Certeau. Further explored in: Jenkins, Henry, *Convergence Culture*. See also publications by Catherine Coker, Christine Handley, Matt Hills and Katherine Larsen in particular.
[205] **Toby Hadoke's Who's Round** #50, 'Russell T Davies: Part 1'.
[206] **Toby Hadoke's Who's Round** #149, 'Russell T Davies: Part 6'.
[207] Davies and Cook, *The Writer's Tale*, p326.
[208] Jenkins, *Textual Poachers*, p81. For further reading, see Alan McKee's critical response to Jenkins' model and the rejection of this binary idea: 'How to tell the difference between production and consumption: a case study in **Doctor Who** fandom' in Gwenllian-Jones, Sara and Robert E Pearson, eds, *Cult Television*, pp167ff.

Because no matter how powerful fandom can be, especially in the digital age... the overwhelming cultural influence of TV production can't be denied.

So, in terms of *Love & Monsters*, what are we looking at? We have a story in which people who symbolise us fans lack the frame of reference to understand the Doctor and, in a larger sense, **Doctor Who**. As decoders, they find themselves forced to interpret things outside of the dominant-hegemonic position that we, the real-life viewers, have access to. They create their own fan works which they are shown both encoding and decoding. Then we see a villain who embodies the type of fan who does have access to the right decoding material, but who uses that information to eliminate the symbolic source material and supplant it with his own interpretive goals. We're also asked to embody Elton's unknown camcorder audience, with Elton as our unreliable encoder, in which we have both a better frame of reference than he does (our knowledge of **Doctor Who**) and a much more limited one (our initial lack of knowledge about Elton's life, and about the Doctor's actions in this specific adventure). Added to that, we have a cast and crew whose decoding as fans has turned into encoding as creators and distributors. And as the big old cherry on top, we have Davies encoding specific things, such as Ursula's transformation as a metaphor for being gay, which are nigh-impossible for us to decode.

Whew.

The end result is that a lot of *Love & Monsters'* audience, quite

---

McKee also examines Marxist views in relation to **Doctor Who**'s fan-creator culture.

understandably, chose what Hall called oppositional decoding – which is fancy academic talk for flipping the author the bird.

Identification With the Characters

No matter how *Love & Monsters* was decoded, **Who**'s viewer base had no trouble recognising LINDA for the fandom that they represent. But the word 'fan' is never said in the episode; and LINDA do nothing to explicitly idolise the Doctor or treat him as a role model. The group has no memorabilia to collect, no conventions to attend and no TV schedule to keep an eye on. Even cosplay, often the go-to visual signifier in stories about fandom (and later seen in the character of Osgood), doesn't make an appearance. It's the symbolic atmosphere of the group, more so than their literal actions, that makes us see these characters for what they portray.

This also means that nothing in the story tells us **how** to decode them. Where one viewer may treat LINDA as 'a flat-out insult to **Doctor Who** fans'[209], the next person may find the little group 'validating like very little else I have ever seen on TV'[210]. We have free rein to see them as empowering or as mocking, as realistic or as bland, as wonderful or as horrid. We can treat them as mirror images of ourselves... or maybe just of that terrible fellow fan from around the block we never liked.

If we choose to go the positive route, there's so much warmth and solidarity in LINDA for us to enjoy. LINDA are clean-cut, well-dressed, good-looking, independent people from different backgrounds coming together to share their common interests. They put effort

---

[209] Aragon, Rick, 'The Worst Doctor Who of All Time. OF ALL TIME!!'.
[210] Holly Boson on twitter, quoted with permission.

into their passions and they lift each other up. The circle of friends showcases all the familiar joys of fandom.

They also each represent aspects of their respective fan demographics that popular media tend to overlook. For example, while fan experience blogs and the 'character shrines' of early 2000s internet culture are commonly run by young women like Ursula, *Love & Monsters* is practically unique in acknowledging this form of female agency. Similarly, Bridget's objective analysis defies harmful stereotypes about female fans being 'overly' affective or downright outgrowing fandom when they hit 30. Bliss as the happy hippy artist embodies a social role which black people are rarely granted on TV, her sculptures transforming the Doctor's white and male-appearing identity to represent her own feelings[211]. Mr Skinner's calm maturity is a far cry from the typical negative portrayal of middle-aged anoraks. Elton shows gentle, attentive and supportive masculinity within the circle. (Although notably, in the original script Elton scolded Ursula with 'not about you' when she dared to talk while filming him[212].) And there's none of the in-fighting, pedantry or poor hygiene that so often defines these groups in reality – meaning that LINDA paint a picture of fandom that's perhaps **more** flattering than expected.

If we go down a more critical path, there's also plenty to dislike. LINDA are gullible, subservient towards Kennedy, and fine with

---

[211] See the Organization of Transformative Works' Fanlore wiki project pages on 'Character Shrine', 'Ageism in Fandom' and 'Race and Fandom' as well as Lamerichs, *Productive Fandom* and Jenkins, *Textual Poachers* for overviews of agency in fan production.
[212] *The Complete History* #53, p84.

becoming manipulative stalkers just to get close to the object of their obsession. The group appears uncoupled from reality, which all the abandoned streets around them signify quite unnervingly. While they're nowhere near the negative caricatures of autistic (or otherwise neurologically atypical) people that some other TV shows present as geeky, *Love & Monsters* still goes out of its way to paint geeks as outsiders. And their final fate as part of the Abzorbaloff makes them, quite literally, gross.

In any case, there's much to be read into LINDA in their kyara-like, barely-defined states. Aside from fandom, they can also symbolise any other group of people who seek each other's company. They can look like our families, our classrooms, our sports clubs or our game night groups. They can be the children who make up their own little fantasy worlds. They can be the old age pensioners we don't talk to enough, who hunger for someone to notice them. They can be the neurologically diverse people in society who find solace in their shared experiences. They can be the theatre nerds who get lost in all their characters. They can be the downtrodden, the outcasts and the strange. They can be the 'pick-up artists' who fuss over archetypes and acronyms, treating the people that they fancy as wild game to hunt. They can be the entitled romantic obsessives who encourage each other's infatuated states. And yes, they can be the ufologist conspiracy nerds, or the cultists, or even our local Bible group – or anyone else grasping at a thread that other people just can't see. With its geeky little cast of stock figures, *Love & Monsters* offers us a wealth of possible interpretations, inviting us to project onto them anything we could want.

Finally, special mention goes to literary scholar Bruce Wyse's opinion that the Abzorbaloff 'ruefully anticipates the insidious encroachment of academic discourse (or cultural studies' research agendas) on the devotion, camaraderie and ingenious enjoyment of **Doctor Who** fandom'[213]. Which just goes to show that *Love & Monsters* has something to identify with for everyone.

A Question of Agency

So.

The blowjob thing.

It's not the first oral sex reference in the series (that accolade goes to a tender moment between Tom Baker and the Erato prop in 1979's *The Creature from the Pit*), nor is it the last. But it's certainly the only one involving a woman's face stuck to a paving slab.

Is it 'appropriate' for **Doctor Who** to include such things? Well, that's a question in two parts...

Firstly, is it appropriate for **Doctor Who** to involve sex jokes at all? The answer isn't as obvious as it once might have been. The 21st century series has an increased focus on relationships, the licensed non-TV material of the Wilderness Years featured erotic content while the show was off the air, and there's a sex-positive vibe pulsing through all of Davies' work. The old 'no hanky-panky in the TARDIS' BBC approach has been thrown right out the window. Modern characters such as Jack Harkness push the boundaries of what can be said and displayed. **Who** is no longer only a kids' show – it's become a celebration of every aspect of life. And sex can be an

---

[213] Wyse, Bruce, 'Cultural Circulation and Circularities in **Doctor Who**: Bardolatry and the Time Vortex of Intertextuality' in *Ruminations, Peregrinations, and Regenerations*, p178.

ingrained part of that for many people. Of course, this also means that for sex-averse viewers (e.g. many on the asexual spectrum, or those who have had negative experiences), their responses may differ significantly from the intention Davies encoded. The scene can feel celebratory or uncomfortable, or even both, depending on each viewer's tastes.

Secondly, is it appropriate for Ursula to have a love life after losing her mobility? That one's easier: a resounding yes. Real-life people with limited mobility face significant shaming for their sexual desires – as does Ursula, from all corners of **Who**'s fandom – which is an issue that needs to be addressed. Because of this, we can interpret Davies' inclusion of these elements as a positive form of social activism, and as an attempt to make audiences think more positively about marginalised relationship forms.

There are many misconceptions around disability and sex (and combinations thereof) which impact the way this scene can be viewed. For example, the false idea that physical disability and sex would somehow be incompatible is disturbingly widespread. Oral sex is also considered more taboo and less 'normal' than other forms of sex in many cultures. And the very act of performing oral sex is too often treated in discourse as being predominantly 'for' the other partner, instead of as something mutually pleasurable. The combination of these factors gives a lot of additional connotations to Ursula's new life.

Davies paints a picture of (sexual) intimacy that is utterly taboo, but asks us to see it as just another part of our favourite show. And with his intention of Ursula as a metaphor for queer relationships, the showrunner invites audiences to question why exactly intimacy between Elton and Ursula would disturb them – and to subsequently adopt more compassionate points of view on queer and/or disabled sex, both within and outside of the fiction[214].

But the question still arises whether Ursula would have enough **agency**. This point comes up time and again in discussions around the episode. Where Davies intended the 'love life' line to be sex-positive, an empowering celebration of physical love that defies hardship and grief, Ursula also ended up being decoded by many as a victim of domestic abuse. And this reasoning doesn't come out of nowhere. The writing does little to present the relationship to us as healthy.

When Elton tells his camcorder audience about their love life he does so without Ursula's consent, which is played off as a joke when she calls him out on it. This demonstrates her helplessness – what else can he do that she would feel uncomfortable with? How could there ever be consequences for his actions? As Jack Graham points out, 'the problem is that he **can** abuse her if he wants because of her extreme physical vulnerability'[215]. In the context of all the unasked for kissing that **Doctor Who** encodes as cute and quirky and romantic, it's not a giant leap to fear Ursula falling victim to that sort of thing as well. And since we've already seen Elton preparing to have sex with a woman as part of stalking said woman's daughter's travelling buddy, it's clear his relationship ethics could use some work.

We're painfully aware of how dependent Ursula will forever be on

---

[214] **Toby Hadoke's Who's Round** #99.
[215] Graham, 'Love & People'.

Elton. Where real-life disabled people may have carers who help them go about their day, Elton's role extends far beyond that – he becomes the only person in Ursula's life. After all, she wouldn't be able to show herself to the world. She's isolated, unable to call for help should she need any, and unable to leave the relationship by herself if she ever wants out. We don't even know for sure whether she's now immortal, which could see her ending up completely alone if Elton were to die of old age[216].

This causes their dynamic to be fundamentally unbalanced, and makes it hard for us to see Ursula as 'obviously an equal partner'[217] no matter what Davies claims. Her placid acceptance of her fate carries with it a horror that the writing declines to address.

The showrunner himself echoes the resignation of his characters in his interviews, describing their ending as happy and complete. He even explicitly links the characters' acceptance of their new lives to the moral economy of fandom, comparing Elton and Ursula's contentment to the ways in which he and other fans choose to tolerate **Doctor Who**'s controversial aspects:

> 'They love each other! They. Love. Each other. [...] And they're very happy together. [...] It's a marvellous moment, hurray for

---

[216] Doctor Who novelist Paul Magrs gave Ursula more agency in his unlicensed short story sequel 'Miss Hawthorne and the Alpaca of Doom'. As a queer Magic Realist author fond of raunchy camp, Magrs was a perfect fit for *Love & Monsters*. He simply described Ursula in her stone slab body shopping, travelling, making new friends, and even defeating the Time Lord Morbius. Once again, a fan-turned-writer added to the complex meta-text of **Doctor Who** to shift its existing mythos into something new.
[217] **Toby Hadoke's Who's Round** #99.

Ursula. It's not the life they want, does anyone? [...] Have you? Who's **got** the life that they want for long? Not many people. But we make the best of it. By watching **Doctor Who**, you have to sit through revelations that he's half-human, and you live with it. You put up with what you've got, and actually make something wonderful of it.'[218]

It's interesting that Davies chooses the Doctor's possible half-human heritage as an example. First mentioned by the eighth Doctor in *Doctor Who* (1996), this issue was left unresolved in the TV series – but was resolved with **countless** explanations and outright retcons in non-TV media by fan-creators, who did not remotely just 'live with it'. The eighth Doctor's legacy is testament to the creative agency of fans, with this incarnation now starring in hundreds of books, comics and audio plays all drawing on his brief TV appearance. The half-human issue ended up explored in the **Eighth Doctor Adventures** novels (and its many spinoffs) which not only challenge this idea with glee, but which also directly spotlight the lore's internal paradoxes, poach the contradictions and dialectically transform them into something new. The fandom chose to 'make something wonderful of it' alright – but through active resistance **as well as** through acceptance.

And so, after much of *Love & Monsters* has explored the power of fans to resist their circumstances, we still end up with the woman 'most likely to fight back' simply tolerating her new life. Ursula's line 'it really is quite peaceful' brings to mind Rosencrantz's statement 'life in a box is better than no life at all' as well as his pre-mortem 'to tell you the truth, I'm relieved' in the sheer absurdity of its

---

[218] **Toby Hadoke's Who's Round** #99.

resignation.

This contradictory finale also perfectly mirrors Brecht's endings, designed to make spectators come up with solutions where the story stops short: the characters' passivity, Elton's untrustworthy narration, the dialogue reaching across the fourth wall to explain that life is so much more than what we're told. Ultimately, Brecht's main goal with this method was to shake audiences out of putting up with anything at all.

It seems Davies didn't write the scene as 'stopping short', though. He considers the characters to have no 'unfinished business'[219] and mocks fans who criticise Ursula's stone slab outcome as though they're homophobic bigots[220]. This attitude contradicts (a) his fan-creator identity and his outspoken love for non-TV stories that fill in the gaps where his own TV episodes leave off[221]; (b) his statements that he doesn't think it's his 'job' to tell fandom how to interpret his episodes, and that he should 'not prescribe to fans what something is, because they'll decide, and history will decide, and you can have too much power' as Executive Producer[222]; and (c) the defiant, never-complete nature of **Doctor Who** itself. But the point is moot – because *Love & Monsters* itself tells us that we as fans have the power to be inspired by contradictions, to rise up against the status quo, and to decode **Doctor Who** any way we like.

Something else that's interesting to examine is the concept of fridging in relation to Ursula, since the story explores Elton's feelings

---

[219] Davies and Cook, *The Writer's Tale*, p675.
[220] **Toby Hadoke's Who's Round** #99.
[221] **Toby Hadoke's Who's Round** #150, 'Russell T Davies: Part 7'.
[222] **Toby Hadoke's Who's Round** #149.

about the whole situation much more than her own. Elton even acknowledges this: he says 'the Doctor saved me' while telling his viewers how Ursula's life was preserved. Such a portrayal of disability doesn't exactly promote audience identification with Ursula. Jack Graham, while ultimately defending the relationship from fans who are bothered by Ursula's immobility, points out that her extreme helplessness and transformation into a literal object still 'could tie in with the perception of "disabled" people as like objects lacking agency'[223].

Indeed, when talking about *Love & Monsters* it's tempting (and, let's be honest, pretty funny) to refer to Ursula **as** the inanimate object she's been smushed onto. But this joke has also become a way for people in fan spaces and criticism circles to feel justified in dehumanising Ursula with open revulsion at her relationship. It's a difficult issue to unpack. Encoding a sex-positive moral about disability into a story tends to be much easier when a character is realistically disabled, ideally played by a disabled person. Such an approach can allow viewers more space to relate the situation to their own frames of reference, to draw positive conclusions about what the sexual relationships of disabled people look like, and to carry a celebratory attitude about sex and disability back with them into their daily lives.

All that said, the 'love life' line **can** just as easily mean a kiss...

Ursula also states that she'll never age, which for some reason she's happy about. If this is vanity, it would make Ursula comparable to Lady Cassandra O'Brien Dot Delta Seventeen from *The End of the*

---

[223] Graham, 'Love & People'.

World (2005) – content to be an immovable, flat face as long as she can stay pretty. Where this perspective made Cassandra an antagonist, and was a valid reason for Rose to mock her, here Davies apparently asks us to accept the same point of view as a happy ending. Ursula's fate additionally parallels that of Borusa and the other petrified faces in *The Five Doctors* (1983), who sought immortality and were punished for their ambition with eternal life trapped in stone form. Why should we see such a fate as horrid in other episodes, but as perfectly okay in *Love & Monsters*? Even if these parallels were completely unintentional, they still add a purpose and a narrative potential to Ursula which the episode leaves unexplored.

But Elton and Ursula's acceptance of their losses can also symbolise the thrill of losing oneself in a fandom, of being drawn into a fictional world. As Lamerichs states, fans can undergo a kind of transformation through their fandom (whether emotionally, or physically e.g. through dress-up and role-play) and in this process the fan often 'prepares to be overwhelmed' and even 'invites a loss of self'[224]. And when we see Ursula staring out from that slab surface, we may choose to see a mirror of our own faces staring unmovingly but happily into **Who**'s world, framed by the flatness of our TV screens.

So, there you go. That's all. That was the story of Elton, and Ursula, and their little gang, and the adventures that they had. And of their 45 minutes spent running, and grieving, and singing, and dancing in the limelight.

---

[224] Lamerichs, *Productive Fandom*, p206.

CONCLUSION

Love & Monsters is a unique part of **Doctor Who**. Its special blend of comedy and alienation leaves its audience guessing every step of the way. Placed between a dramatic tale starring Satan and a little fairy tale about childhood fears, the episode is in a fantastic position to wrong-foot audiences and to turn people's understanding of the series on its head.

It's a story in which we, the audience, are characters. And one in which Davies appears threaded throughout the plot as well, if not as explicitly. The showrunner tells us that he's part of the fandom, like LINDA; he's a super-fan lording over other fans, like the Abzorbaloff; and he plays inscrutable games with us, takes us on journeys we may not want to go on and always stays just out of reach, like the Doctor. As viewers, we're invited to question the very nature of the show, including the writing itself. And the fandom gets to have the final word, embodied by a geeky little nobody – and no-one else.

Whatever Davies explicitly or implicitly encoded into the episode, we're free to make the whole thing mean whatever we want it to. There are so many layers of narrative and metafictionality to peel back in *Love & Monsters* that the communication between the author and the audience becomes more than just straightforward storytelling. Even the episode itself can be ascribed an attitude, as Jack Graham states: 'The episode could be looked at as a commodity critiquing some ways in which it is consumed, favouring others'[225].

---

[225] Graham, Jack, personal correspondence.

But the emotional core of the story rings loud and clear: namely, that **Doctor Who** is a mythology made for fans, by fans, and that we all continually shape the franchise into something new. The Doctor's adventures give us all the elements that make a story tick, which we can apply to our own lives and our own world-crafting any way we like – comedy and horror, mundanity and grief, friendship and joy, awkwardness and callous mockery, hypocrisy and death. And yes, maybe a bit of love too, and some big old rubber-suit monsters.

Let's take one final look at Brecht. He designed his plays to be alienating, showing his audiences tales that made the ordinary seem wonderfully strange. But spectators didn't always catch on to his encoding. And so, he re-imagined his *Threepenny Opera* as the *Threepenny Novel* to alienate the storytelling even further, with a text-only take on the whole thing – shown without its famous actors, without its theatrical glamour, without its props or its music or its pretty lights.

Such a radical re-imagining of a story, stripped bare of all its bells and whistles, has the power to jolt audiences awake and to make them consider whole new points of view. Just like Brecht gave us a story from the sidelines, Davies here stripped **Doctor Who** bare of all its space adventure glamour and showed us the tiny, befuddled, utterly mundane lives of those who are left behind. And just for a moment, whether by Fewkoombey's side or by Elton's, we could find ourselves strangers on the outside looking in.

Maybe as you're reading this, a text-only Target *Love & Monsters* novelisation will have seen the light of day as well. And maybe Ursula's transformation will be obviously queer this time around, or maybe the Abzorbaloff will remind us a bit more of some particularly obnoxious fan. Or maybe not. Because the world is changing and transforming too, making room for new lessons that can be taught, new fannish circles of new geeks hungry to seize the reins. Maybe this strange adventure that's been absorbed into fandom's consciousness can be re-imagined to tell another story altogether. But it will always have been this wonderful little side-step in the Doctor's life. And as fans, we have the opportunity to look beyond the episode's awkwardness and camp – and to celebrate *Love & Monsters* for all that it is.

Because it's so much darker...

...and so much madder...

...and, y'know, it's got a blowjob joke and everything.

Afterword

When I announced that I'd be writing a book on *Love & Monsters*, most people thought I'd gone bananas. My friend Ossi had my favourite response – one of **pity**, that I'd 'been given the worst episode in the entire show!' I'll always remember his face when I told him I'd picked it myself.

I adore *Love & Monsters*. I really do. It's such a heartfelt love letter to the fandom. No other episode in the TV series at the time was as daring, as far removed from the normal format. I'm very grateful that I was invited to talk about it in this book. And I'm equally grateful to Professor Jürgen Schutte of the Free University of Berlin, who taught me about Brecht with exceptional insight, showing me how beautifully analytical writing can combine with just being a big old nerd.

Every **Doctor Who** story deserves to be watched twice, but *Love & Monsters* more than any other. Because once we know what Elton knows, we're no longer the outsiders that we were when we first embodied his camcorder audience. And we can experience the episode from yet another point of view – that of the time traveller, who can re-wind it and re-watch it and discover new meaning in old tales. When you see it again, I hope my little book will have convinced you to look for all the love and warmth that's pulsing through this story.

Two years after *Love & Monsters* aired, a different adventure made its way into fandom's global consciousness. Like Elton, that story's hero was an awkward geek trying clumsily to impress a villain, and chatting away on his vlog, and singing, and stalking a lady he'd met at the launderette.

Unlike Elton, Dr. Horrible won a Hugo.

Ah well.

BIBLIOGRAPHY
Books

Adams, Douglas, *The Restaurant at the End of the Universe*. 1980. New York, Random House Publishing Group, 2008. ISBN 9780307497567.

Arnold, Jon, *Rose*. **The Black Archive** #1. Edinburgh, Obverse Books, 2016. ISBN 9781909031371.

Arnold, Jon, *The Eleventh Hour*. **The Black Archive** #19. Edinburgh, Obverse Books, 2016. ISBN 9781909031685.

Barnett, David, *Brecht in Practice: Theatre, Theory and Performance*. London, Bloomsbury Publishing, 2014. ISBN 9781408186022.

Bennett, Lucy and Paul Booth, eds, *Seeing Fans: Representations of Fandom in Media*. London, Bloomsbury Publishing, 2016. ISBN 9781501318450.

Booth, Paul, *Playing Fans: Negotiating Fandom and Media in the Digital Age*. Iowa City, University Of Iowa Press, 2015. ISBN 9781609383190.

Booy, Miles, *Love and Monsters*. London, IB Tauris & Co. Ltd., 2012. ISBN 9781848854796.

Brecht, Bertolt and Elisabeth Hauptmann, *The Threepenny Opera (Die Dreigroschenoper)*. Desmond I. Vesey and Eric Bentley, trans, New York, Grove Press, 1994. ISBN 9780802150394.

Brecht, Bertolt, *Threepenny Novel (Dreigroschenroman)*. 1934. Desmond I Vesey, Christopher Isherwood, trans, New York, Grove Press, 1956. ISBN 9789997405029.

Cornell, Paul, *Human Nature*. **Doctor Who: The New Adventures**. London, Virgin Publishing Ltd, 1995. ISBN 9780426204435.Da Costa, Portia, *The Stranger*. 1997. London, Virgin Books, 2012. ISBN 9780352346759.

Davies, Russell T, *Rose*. **Doctor Who: Target Collection**. London, BBC Books, , 2018. ISBN 9781785943263.

Davies, Russell T and Benjamin Cook, *The Writer's Tale: The Final Chapter.* London, BBC Books, 2010. ISBN 9781846078613.

De Certeau, Michel, *The Practice of Everyday Life* (*L'Invention du quotidien, 1. : Arts de faire*). 1980. Steven Rendall, trans, Berkeley, Los Angeles, London, University of California Press, 1984. ISBN 9780520271456.

Derrida, Jacques, *Archive Fever: A Freudian Impression* (*Mal d'Archive: Une Impression Freudienne*). 1995. Eric Prenowitz, trans, Chicago and London, The University of Chicago Press, 1996. ISBN 0226143678.

Deuze, Mark, *Media Work*. Cambridge, Polity Press, 2007. ISBN 9780745639253.

Douglas, Stuart, ed, *A Target for Tommy*. Edinburgh, Obverse Books, 2016.

Magrs, Paul, 'Miss Hawthorne and the Alpaca of Doom'.

During, Simon, ed, *The Cultural Studies Reader*. London, Psychology Press, 1999. ISBN 9780415374132.

Hall, Stuart, 'Encoding, decoding'.

Engels, Friedrich and Karl Marx: *Manifest der Kommunistischen Partei* ['Manifesto of the Communist Party'], 1848. Stuttgart, Phillip

Reclam jun. Verlag, 2005. ISBN 3150083230.

Gay, John, *The Beggar's Opera*. Mineola, Dover Publications Inc., 2000. ISBN 9780486408880.

Gellert, Inge, Werner Hecht, Marianne Conrad, Sigmar Gerund and Benno Slupianek, eds, *Bertolt Brecht: Schriften 2* ['Writings 2']. **Werke. Große kommentierte Berliner und Frankfurter Ausgabe** #22. Berlin and Weimar, Aufbau Verlag and Frankfurt am Main, Suhrkamp Verlag, 1993. ISBN 9783518400821.

>Brecht, Bertolt, '[Aufgeben der Einfühlung]' ['[Letting Go of Immersion]'].

>Brecht, Bertolt, 'Fünf Schwierigkeiten beim Schreiben der Wahrheit' ['Five Difficulties in Writing the Truth'].

>Brecht, Bertolt, 'Über experimentelles Theater' ['On Experimental Theatre'].

Gwenllian-Jones, Sara and Robert E. Pearson, eds, *Cult Television*. Minneapolis, University of Minnesota Press, 2004. ISBN 9780816638314.

>McKee, Alan, 'How to tell the difference between production and consumption: a case study in Doctor Who fandom'.

Hansen, Christopher J, ed, *Ruminations, Peregrinations, and Regenerations: A Critical Approach to Doctor Who*. Newcastle upon Tyne, Cambridge Scholars Publishing, 2010. ISBN 9781443820844.

>Basu, Balaka, 'When Worlds Continue: The Doctor's Adventures in Fandom and Metatextuality'.

>Cordone, Michelle and John Cordone, 'Who is the Doctor? The Meta-Narrative of **Doctor Who**'.

McNaughton, Douglas, 'Regeneration of a Brand: The Fan Audience and the 2005 **Doctor Who** Revival'.

Vasquez, Joshua, 'The Moral Economy of **Doctor Who**: Forgiving Fans and the Objects of Their Devotion'.

Wyse, Bruce, 'Cultural Circulation and Circularities in **Doctor Who**: Bardolatry and the Time Vortex of Intertextuality'.

Heath, Stephen, ed/trans, *Image, Music, Text*. London, FontanaPress, 1983. ISBN 9780006861355.

Barthes, Roland, 'From Work to Text'.

Barthes, Roland, 'The Death of the Author'.

Hecht, Werner, Marianne Conrad, Sigmar Gerund and Benno Slupianek, eds, *Bertolt Brecht: Schriften 1* ['Writings 1']. **Werke. Große kommentierte Berliner und Frankfurter Ausgabe** #21. Berlin and Weimar, Aufbau Verlag and Frankfurt am Main, Suhrkamp Verlag, 1992. ISBN 9783518400814.

Brecht, Bertolt, 'Der Dreigroschenprozess' ['The Threepenny Process'].

Brecht, Bertolt, 'Dialektische Kritik' ['Dialectical Criticism'].

Brecht, Bertolt, 'Lehre von eingreifenden Sätzen (praktiklen Definitionen)' ['Teachings of engaging Sentences (feasible Definitions)'].

Hecht, Werner and Marianne Conrad, eds, *Bertolt Brecht: Schriften 5* ['Writings 5']. **Werke. Große kommentierte Berliner und Frankfurter Ausgabe** #21. Berlin and Weimar, Aufbau Verlag and Frankfurt am Main, Suhrkamp Verlag, 1994. ISBN 9783518400852.

Brecht, Bertolt, 'Couragemodell 1949' ['Couragemodel 1949'].

Hecht, Werner, Jan Knopf, Werner Mittenzwei and Klaus-Detlef Müller, eds, *Bertolt Brecht: Stücke 3* ['Plays 3']. **Werke. Große kommentierte Berliner und Frankfurter Ausgabe** #3. Berlin and Weimar, Aufbau Verlag and Frankfurt am Main, Suhrkamp Verlag, 1988. ISBN 9783518400630.

Brecht, Bertolt, *Die Ausnahme und die* Regel ['The Exception and the Rule'].

Helbig, Jörg, *Intertextualität und* Markierung ['Intertextuality and Marking']. Heidelberg, Universitätsverlag Winter GmbH, 1996. ISBN 9783825303402.

Hickman, Clayton, ed, *Doctor Who Annual 2006*. Tunbridge Wells, Panini UK Ltd, 2005. ISBN 1904419739.

Davies, Russell T, 'Meet Rose'.

Hills, Matt, *Fan Cultures*. New York, Routledge, 2002. ISBN 9780415240253.

Itō, Gō, *TEZUKA is Dead: Postmodernist and Modernist Approaches to Japanese Manga* (*Tezuka izu deddo: hirakareta manga hyōgenron e*). Tokyo, NTT Shuppan, 2005. ISBN 9784757141292.

Jenkins, Henry, *Convergence Culture: Where Old and New Media Collide*. New York and London, New York University Press, 2006. ISBN 9780814742815.

Jenkins, Henry and John Tulloch, *Science Fiction Audiences: Watching Star Trek and Doctor Who*. New York, Routledge, 1995. ISBN 9780415061414.

Jenkins, Henry, *Textual Poachers: Television Fans & Participatory Culture*. 1992. 2nd (revised) edition. New York, Routledge, 2012. ISBN 9780415533294.

Knopf, Jan, *Bertolt Brecht*. Ditzingen, Philipp Reclam jun. GmbH & Co. KG, 2000. ISBN 9783150176191.

Knopf, Jan, Michael Duchardt, Ute Liebig and Brigitte Bergheim, eds, *Bertolt Brecht: Prosa 3* ['Prose 3']. **Werke. Große kommentierte Berliner und Frankfurter Ausgabe** #18. Berlin and Weimar, Aufbau Verlag and Frankfurt am Main, Suhrkamp Verlag, 1995. ISBN 9783518400784.

Brecht, Bertolt, 'Rechtsprechung' ['Jurisdiction'].

Kraft, Peter, Marianne Conrad, Sigmar Gerund and Benno Slupianek, eds, *Bertolt Brecht: Schriften 4* ['Writings 4']. **Werke. Große kommentierte Berliner und Frankfurter Ausgabe** #24. Berlin and Weimar, Aufbau Verlag and Frankfurt am Main, Suhrkamp Verlag, 1991. ISBN 9783518400241.

Brecht, Bertolt, 'Anmerkungen zur *Dreigroschenoper*' ['Notes on the "Threepenny Opera"'].

Brecht, Bertolt, 'Zu *Die Mutter*' ['On "The Mother"'].

Brecht, Bertolt, 'Zu *Trommeln in der Nacht*' ['On "Drums in the Night"'].

Brecht, Bertolt and Peter Suhrkamp, 'Anmerkungen zur Oper *Aufstieg und Fall der Stadt Mahagonny*' ['Notes on the opera "Rise and Fall of the City of Mahagonny"'].

Lamerichs, Nicolle, *Productive Fandom: Intermediality and Affective Reception in Fan Cultures*. 2014. 2nd (revised) edition. Amsterdam,

Amsterdam University Press, 2018. ISBN 9789048528318.

Larsen, Katherine and Lynn Zubernis, *Fan Culture: Theory/Practice*. Newcastle upon Tyne, Cambridge Scholars Publishing, 2012. ISBN 9781443837835.

Hills, Matt, '"Proper Distance" in the Ethical Positioning of Scholar-Fandoms: Between Academics' and Fans' Moral Economies?'.

Le Fanu, Joseph Sheridan, *Carmilla*. 1871-72. London, Hesperus Press Ltd, 2013. ISBN 9781843914723.

Orman, Kate, *Pyramids of Mars*. **The Black Archive** #12. Edinburgh, Obverse Books, 2017. ISBN 9781909031579.

Orthia, Lindy, ed, *Doctor Who and Race*. Bristol, Intellect Books, 2013. ISBN 9781783200368.

Rodebaugh, Thomas, *The Face of Evil*. **The Black Archive** #27. Edinburgh, Obverse Books, 2019. ISBN 9781909031814.

Rose, Lloyd, *Camera Obscura*. **Doctor Who: The Eighth Doctor Adventures**. London, BBC Books, 2002. ISBN 9780563538578.

Russell, Gary, **Doctor Who**: *The Inside Story – The Official Guide to Series 1 and 2*. London, BBC Books, 2006. ISBN 9780563486497.

Shakespeare, William, *Hamlet*. Oxford, Oxford University Press, 2009. ISBN 9780199535811.

Schutte, Jürgen, *Einführung in die Literaturinterpretation* ['Introduction to Interpreting Literature']. 1985. 5th (revised) edition. Stuttgart, J. B. Metzlersche Verlagsbuchhandlung; Stuttgart, Carl Ernst Poeschel Verlag, 2005. ISBN 9783476152176.

Shklovsky, Viktor, *Theory of Prose* (*O teorii prozy*). 1925. Benjamin Sher, trans, Champaign and London, Dalkey Archive Press, 1990. ISBN 0916583546.

Southall, JR, ed, *Hating to Love: Re-Evaluating the 52 Worst Doctor Who Stories of All Time*. Exeter, Watching Books, 2017. ISBN 9781542635714.

Arnold, Jon, 'Love & Monsters'.

Stoker, Bram, *Dracula*. 1897. London, Penguin Books, 2003. ISBN 9780141439846.

Stoppard, Tom, *Rosencrantz and Guildenstern Are Dead*. London, Faber and Faber, 1967. ISBN 9780571081820

Tulloch, John and Manuel Alvarado, **Doctor Who**: *The Unfolding Text*. New York, St Martins Press, 1984. ISBN 9780312214807.

Wallburg, Barbara, Marianne Conrad, Sigmar Gerund, Werner Hecht and Benno Slupianek, *Bertolt Brecht: Schriften 3* ['Writings 3']. **Werke. Große kommentierte Berliner und Frankfurter Ausgabe** #23. Berlin and Weimar, Aufbau Verlag and Frankfurt am Main, Suhrkamp Verlag, 1993. ISBN 9783518400838.

Brecht, Bertolt, 'Kleines Organon für das Theater' ['Short Organum for the Theatre'].

Brecht, Bertolt, 'Nachträge zum "Kleinen Organon"' ['Addenda to the "Short Organum"'].

Willett, Jon, ed/trans, *Brecht on Theatre*. New York, Hill and Wang, 1964. ISBN 9780809005420.

Wright, Mark, ed, **Doctor Who**: *The Complete History Volume 53*. Tunbridge Wells, Panini UK Ltd, 2016. ISBN 97762057604029.

Pixley, Andrew, 'Love & Monsters'.

Periodicals

Doctor Who Magazine (DWM). Marvel UK, Panini, BBC, 1979-.

> Morrison, Grant, 'The World Shapers'. DWM #127-129, cover dates August-October 1987.

> Cook, Benjamin, 'Leader Of The Gang'. DWM #386, cover date September 2007.

> Davies, Russell T, 'Second Sight'. DWM Special Editions #14, cover date November 2006.

Andrejevic, Mark, 'Watching Television Without Pity: The Productivity of Online Fans'. *Television & New Media* #9(1), January 2008.

Television

Blue Peter. BBC, 1958-.

> Editions broadcast 14 December 1967, 17 August 2005

Bob & Rose. Red Production Company, 2001.

Buffy the Vampire Slayer. Mutant Enemy Productions, Sandollar Television, Kuzui Enterprises, 20th Century Fox Television. 1997-2003.

> *The Zeppo*, 1999.

> *The Body*, 2001.

Clocking Off. Red Production Company, 2000-03.

Doctor Who. BBC, 1963-.

Love & Monsters commentary with Russell T Davies, Phil Collinson, Susie Liggat. DVD extra, 2006.

Love & Monsters commentary, The Complete Second Series edition with Dan Zeff, Camille Coduri, Julie Gardner. DVD extra, 2009.

Doctor Who Confidential. BBC, 2005-11.

The New World of Who, 2006.

The Hitchhiker's Guide to the Galaxy. BBC, 1981.

Episode 2, 1981.

Linda Green. Red Production Company, 2001-02.

Star Trek: The Next Generation. Paramount Domestic Television, 1987-94.

Lower Decks, 1994.

Terry Pratchett's Hogfather, Sky One, 2006.

The Sarah Jane Adventures. BBC, 2007-11.

Revenge of the Slitheen, 2007.

The Gift, 2009.

Torchwood. BBC Wales, BBC Worldwide, Canadian Broadcasting Corporation, Starz Entertainment, 2006-11.

Random Shoes, 2006.

Reset, 2008.

Exit Wounds, 2008.

Why Don't You ...? BBC, 1973-95.

Film

Baggs, Bill, dir, **The Stranger**. BBV, 1991-95.

Barry, Christopher, dir, *Downtime*. Reeltime Pictures, 1995.

Clements, Ron and John Musker, dir, *The Little Mermaid*. Walt Disney Pictures, Walt Disney Feature Animation, 1989.

Stoppard, Tom, dir, *Rosencrantz & Guildenstern Are Dead*. Brandenberg, WNET Channel 13 New York, 1990.

Whedon, Joss, *Dr Horrible's Sing-Along Blog*. Mutant Enemy Productions, 2008.

Web

'20 Questions With...David Tennant'. Team Tennant, 2003. http://www.team-tennant.com/interview/id103.html. Accessed 21 January 2019.

'Ageism in Fandom'. Fanlore. https://fanlore.org/wiki/Ageism_in_Fandom. Accessed 21 January 2019.

'BBC wins battle over Dalek book'. BBC, 16 April 2008. http://news.bbc.co.uk/2/hi/entertainment/7350858.stm. Accessed 21 January 2019.

'Character Shrine'. Fanlore. https://fanlore.org/wiki/Character_Shrine. Accessed 21 January 2019.

'Hoax This!' http://www.whoisdoctorwho.co.uk/index6.shtml. Who Is Doctor Who?, BBC. Accessed 21 January 2019.

'Introduction to The Web of Fear'. BBC.

http://www.bbc.co.uk/doctorwho/classic/photonovels/weboffear/intro.shtml. Accessed 21 January 2019.

'Lower-Deck Episode'. TV Tropes. http://tvtropes.org/pmwiki/pmwiki.php/Main/LowerDeckEpisode. Accessed 21 January 2019.Accessed 21 January 2019.

'Race and Fandom'. Fanlore. https://fanlore.org/wiki/Race_and_Fandom. Accessed 21 January 2019.

'The Organization for Transformative Works'. http://www.transformativeworks.org. Accessed 21 January 2019.

'Women in Refrigerators'. March 1999. http://www.lby3.com/wir. Accessed 21 January 2019.

Boson, Holly, @fireh9lly. Twitter, 05 February 2018. https://twitter.com/fireh9lly/status/960648531915759621. Accessed 21 January 2019.

Aragon, Rick, 'The Worst **Doctor Who** of All Time. OF ALL TIME!'. Gallifrey Exile, 05 February 2014. http://gallifreyexile.blogspot.nl/2014/02/the-worst-doctor-who-of-all-time-of-all.html. Accessed 21 January 2019.

Arnopp, Jason, 'Steven Moffat On Writing'. Jason Arnopp's Bloggery Pokery, 29 June 2008. http://jasonarnopp.blogspot.co.uk/2008/06/steven-moffat-on-writing.html. Accessed 21 January 2019.

Baker, Colin, 'I was the Doctor and I'm over the moon that at last we have a female lead'. The Guardian, 2017. https://www.theguardian.com/commentisfree/2017/jul/17/colin-baker-doctor-who-female-lead-doctor-jodie-whittaker-inspire-fans. Accessed 21 January 2019.

Bone, Christian, 'David Tennant Reveals How He Was Offered The Role Of Doctor Who'. We Got This Covered, July 2018. https://wegotthiscovered.com/tv/david-tennant-reveals-offered-doctor-who. Accessed 21 January 2019.

Emily, 'Another c2e2 video that was hidden on my camera. Peter Davison tells the story of how he first met David Tennant.'. Tumblr, 13 May 2013. http://postcardsfromtheoryland.tumblr.com/post/51838991320. Accessed 21 January 2019.

Graham, Jack, 'Love & People'. Shabogan Graffiti, 25 October 2013. http://shabogangraffiti.blogspot.nl/2013/10/love-people.html. Accessed 21 January 2019.

Hadoke, Toby, 'Russell T Davies: Part 1'. **Toby Hadoke's Who's Round** #50. Big Finish Productions, 21 March 2014. https://www.bigfinish.com/releases/v/toby-hadoke-s-who-s-round-50---russell-t-davies-part-1-1062. Accessed 21 January 2019.

Hadoke, Toby, 'Russell T Davies: Part 2'. **Toby Hadoke's Who's Round** #54. Big Finish Productions, 4 April 2014. https://www.bigfinish.com/releases/v/toby-hadoke-s-who-s-round-54---russell-t-davies-part-2-1068. Accessed 21 January 2019.

Hadoke, Toby, 'Russell T Davies: Part 3'. **Toby Hadoke's Who's Round** #59. Big Finish Productions, 28 April 2014. https://www.bigfinish.com/releases/v/toby-hadoke-s-who-s-round-59---russell-t-davies-part-3-1073. Accessed 21 January 2019.

Hadoke, Toby, 'Russell T Davies: Part 4'. **Toby Hadoke's Who's**

Round #99. Big Finish Productions, 23 December 2014. https://www.bigfinish.com/releases/v/toby-hadoke-s-who-s-round-99---russell-t-davies-part-4-1197. Accessed 21 January 2019.

Hadoke, Toby, 'Russell T Davies: Part 5'. **Toby Hadoke's Who's Round** #124. Big Finish Productions, 12 June 2015. https://www.bigfinish.com/releases/v/toby-hadoke-s-who-s-round-124---russell-t-davies-part-5-1332. Accessed 21 January 2019.

Hadoke, Toby, 'Russell T Davies: Part 6'. **Toby Hadoke's Who's Round** #149. Big Finish Productions, 4 December 2015. https://www.bigfinish.com/releases/v/toby-hadoke-s-who-s-round-149---russell-t-davies-part-6-1423. Accessed 21 January 2019.

Hadoke, Toby, 'Russell T Davies: Part 7'. **Toby Hadoke's Who's Round** #150. Big Finish Productions, 10 December 2015. https://www.bigfinish.com/releases/v/toby-hadoke-s-who-s-round-150---russell-t-davies-part-7-1424. Accessed 21 January 2019.

Haque, Ahsan, '**Doctor Who**: "Love & Monsters" Review', IGN, 11 December 2006, https://uk.ign.com/articles/2006/12/11/doctor-who-love-monsters-review. Accessed 5 January 2019

Johnston, Connor, 'INTERVIEW: BILLY HANSHAW ON SERIES 8'S TITLE SEQUENCE'. Doctor Who TV, 01 September 2014. http://www.doctorwhotv.co.uk/interview-billy-hanshaw-on-series-8s-title-sequence-66152.htm. Accessed 21 January 2019.

Mammone, Rob, 'Gary Russell talks about the **Audio Visuals**'. Justyce. http://justyce.org/gary-russell-interview.html. Accessed 21 January 2019.

Morimoto, Lori, 'Lecture 1'. Patreon, 01 September 2017. https://www.patreon.com/posts/lecture-1-and-in-14112178.

Accessed 21 January 2019.

Morimoto, Lori, 'Lecture 2'. Patreon, 07 October 2017. https://www.patreon.com/posts/before-fan-14743962. Accessed 21 January 2019.

Murray, Noel, 'Buffy The Vampire Slayer: *The Zeppo / Bad Girls / Consequences*'. The A.V. Club, 26 June 2009. https://tv.avclub.com/buffy-the-vampire-slayer-the-zeppo-bad-girls-1798206493. Accessed 21 January 2019.

Pixley, Andrew, 'HIDDEN TREASURE: The Compulsion to Research **Doctor Who'**. Earthbound Timelords, 02 December 2000. http://homepages.bw.edu/~jcurtis/Pixley_1.htm. Accessed 21 January 2019.

Roberts, Gareth, *Tardisode 10*. BBC, 03 June 2006. https://archive.org/search.php?query=http%3A%2F%2Fwww.bbc.co.uk%2Fdoctorwho%2Fram%2Fbb%2Ftardisode10_16x9_bb.asx. Accessed 21 January 2019.

Sandifer, Elizabeth, 'Their Little Groups (*Love & Monsters*)'. Eruditorum Press, 2013. http://www.eruditorumpress.com/blog/their-little-groups-love-and-monsters. Accessed 21 January 2019.Seavey, John, 'Craig Hinton'. The **Doctor Who** Ratings Guide, 01 April 2013. http://www.pagefillers.com/dwrg/hinton.htm. Accessed 21 January 2019.

Sullivan, Shannon Patrick, '*Love & Monsters*'. Shannon Patrick Sullivan, 06 July 2014. http://www.shannonsullivan.com/drwho/serials/2006j.html. Accessed 21 January 2019.

Wilkins, Alasdair, '**Doctor Who**: *Love & Monsters / Fear Her*'. The A.V. Club, 23 February 2014. https://tv.avclub.com/doctor-who-love-and-monsters-fear-her-1798179595. Accessed 21 January 2019.

Wood, Jennifer M, '15 Surprising Facts About David Tennant'. Mental Floss, 18 April 2018. http://mentalfloss.com/article/540376/facts-about-david-tennant-doctor-who. Accessed 21 January 2019.

ACKNOWLEDGEMENTS

Niki Haringsma would like to thank:

Sonja Bergström; Jacob Black; William Shaw; Christine Grit; Yann Chen; Nicolle Lamerichs; James Bojaciuk; Anne-Laure Tuduri; Oswald de Bruin; Noortje Wijkamp; Kas de Man; Nate Bumber; Jack Guidera; James Maddox; Charles Whitt; Kevin Burnard; Alex Marchon; Luis Galván-Ferretíz; Marcel Penke; Johannes Chazot; Jon Arnold; Ian Potter; Roy Gill; Thomas Rodebaugh; Alan Stevens; Athenodora Cat; Meghan Blake; Geoffrey Lourens; Jack Graham; Robert Smith?; Jürgen Schutte; Seumas MacDonald (the Red Wizard of Ûr); Gabriel Titchiner; Erik Woldhuis; Simon Otjes; Linda Muusses; Edin Najetovic; László Huszár; Iskander Terence Gitan Ilias Dezentje; Tamara Beij; Pauline Tubbergen; Louise Tubbergen; Erik Toffolo; Charlotte Kamminga; the rest of the bar gang; Paul Simpson; Rodo & Bella; Stuart Douglas; Philip Purser-Hallard; the Bumblebee Conspiracy; my family; Colin the sheep; Catherine the rabbit; and everyone else who listened to me ramble about silly monsters at ungodly hours.

And Andrew Pixley – though we've never met – for being the best kind of fan in all the world.

BIOGRAPHY

Niki Haringsma is a Dutch writer, artist and editor with a degree in German literature.

After years of resisting the series' siren call, Niki finally fell in love with **Doctor Who** in 2012 and never stopped falling. You can find Niki's fiction for Obverse Books in *Faction Paradox: The Book of the Peace*, and lots more **Who**-related nerdery (comics, short stories and non-fiction) scattered across charity anthologies. Niki's artwork is published at https://nikiharingsma.wordpress.com and mostly involves floaty things poking each other a lot.

When not busy daydreaming about queer sci-fi geeks, Niki also tweets over at @nikisketches.

Coming Soon

The Black Archive #29: The Impossible Astronaut / Day of the Moon by John Toon

The Black Archive #30: The Dalek Invasion of Earth by Jonathan Morris

The Black Archive #31: Warriors' Gate by Frank Collins

The Black Archive #32: The Romans by Jacob Edwards

The Black Archive #33: Horror of Fang Rock by Matthew Guerreri

The Black Archive #34: Battlefield by Philip Purser-Hallard

The Black Archive #35: Timelash by Phil Pascoe

The Black Archive #36: Listen by Dewi Small

The Black Archive #37: Kerblam! by Naomi Jacobs and Thomas Rodebaugh

The Black Archive #38: The Underwater Menace by James Cooray Smith

The Black Archive #39: The Sound of Drums / Last of the Time Lords by James Mortimer

The Black Archive #40: The Silurians by Robert Smith?

The Black Archive #41: Vengeance on Varos by Jonathan Dennis

The Black Archive #42: The Rings of Akhaten by William Shaw

The Black Archive #43: The Robots of Death by Fiona Moore

The Black Archive #44: The Pandorica Opens / The Big Bang by Philip Bates

The Black Archive #45: The Unquiet Dead by Erin Horáková

The Black Archive #46: The Awakening by David Powell

The Black Archive #47: The Stones of Blood by Katrin Thier

The Black Archive #48: The Tenth Planet by Michael Seely

The Black Archive #49: Arachnids in the UK by Samuel Maleski

The Black Archive #50: The Day of the Doctor by Alasdair Stuart

The Black Archive #50A: The Night of the Doctor by James Cooray Smith